STORIES OF THE EAST
FROM HERODOTUS

DARIUS

STORIES OF THE EAST
FROM HERODOTUS

BY

ALFRED J. CHURCH

with illustrations from

Ancient Frescoes and Sculptures

YESTERDAY'S CLASSICS
CHAPEL HILL, NORTH CAROLINA

This edition, first published in 2009 by Yesterday's Classics, an imprint of Yesterday's Classics, LLC, is an unabridged republication of the text originally published by Scribner and Welford in 1881. For the complete listing of the books that are published by Yesterday's Classics, please visit www.yesterdaysclassics.com. Yesterday's Classics is the publishing arm of the Baldwin Online Children's Literature Project which presents the complete text of hundreds of classic books for children at www.mainlesson.com.

ISBN-10: 1-59915-386-6

ISBN-13: 978-1-59915-386-5

Yesterday's Classics, LLC
PO Box 3418
Chapel Hill, NC 27515

TO

WILLIAM AND MARIA OVEREND,

KINDEST OF FRIENDS,
THIS BOOK IS DEDICATED.

PREFACE

In these stories I have kept as close to my original as I could, but I do not profess to have translated it. Of course, nothing like criticism or correction has been attempted.

I should be sorry that readers who are not acquainted with the work of the "Father of History" should carry away from this book the impression that he is nothing more than a credulous and gossiping teller of stories. That he was often deceived, and that he writes with a simplicity which is quite remote from our ways of thinking, is manifest; but those who know him best are aware that he was nevertheless a shrewd and painstaking observer, whose credit has been distinctly increased by the discoveries of modern times.

I wish to express my sincere gratitude to my relative, Miss E. L. Seeley, for the pains which she has bestowed on the illustrations to this volume.

HADLEY GREEN,
September 30, 1880

CONTENTS

CHAPTER I

THE STORY OF KING CRŒSUS

CRŒSUS, the son of Alyattes, began to reign over Lydia, being thirty and five years old. This Crœsus made war upon all the Greeks that dwelt in the western parts of Asia, seeking some occasion of quarrel with every city. And if he could find some great matter, he used it gladly; but if not, a little thing would serve his turn. Now, the first of all the cities which he fought against was Ephesus; and when the Ephesians were besieged by him they offered their city as an offering to the goddess Artemis, fastening a rope to the wall from her temple. (The space between the temple and the wall was seven furlongs.) All the cities of the Greeks that are on the mainland did Crœsus subdue, so that they paid tribute to him. And when he had ended this business, he purposed in his heart to build ships, and to make war on the Greeks that dwelt in the islands. But when all things were now ready for the building of the ships, there came to Sardis a certain Greek, a man renowned for wisdom. Some say that this Greek was Bias, the wise man of Priene, and some that he was Pittacus of Mitylene. This Greek caused Crœsus to cease from his shipbuilding, for when the King would know whether

1

he had any news from Greece, he said to him, "O King, the islanders are buying ten thousand horses, that they may set riders upon them, and so march against thee and thy city of Sardis." When Crœsus heard this he was glad, hoping that the man spake truth, and said, "Now may the Gods put this into the hearts of the islanders, that they should make war with horses against the sons of the Lydians." Then the Greek answered and said, "O King, I see that thou prayest with all thy heart that thou mayest find the islanders coming against thee here on the mainland with horses, and verily thou doest well. What then dost thou think that the islanders pray for now that they know thee to be building ships? Surely that they may find the Lydians coming against them on the sea, that so they may take vengeance on thee for their brethren on the mainland, whom thou hast brought into slavery." This saying pleased King Crœsus mightily; and because the Greek seemed to him to speak truly, he ceased straightway from his shipbuilding, and made alliance with the Greeks that dwelt in the islands.

Now after certain years, when all Asia that lieth to the westward of the river Halys had been subdued by Crœsus (only Lydia and Cilicia were not subdued), and his kingdom flourished with great wealth and honour, there came to Sardis all the wise men of the Greeks, as many as there were in those days. But the greatest of all that came was Solon of Athens. This Solon had made laws for the Athenians, for they would have him make them, and afterwards he dwelt abroad for ten years. And he said that he did this that he might see foreign countries; but in truth he departed that he might not be compelled to change any of the laws that he had made. For the Athenians themselves could not change any, having bound themselves with great oaths to Solon, that they would live for the space of ten years under the laws which he had made for them.

Solon therefore came to Sardis, and Crœsus entertained him in his palace. And on the third or fourth day after his coming the King commanded his servants that they should show Solon all the royal treasures. So the servants showed him all the things that the King possessed, a very great store of riches. And when he had seen everything and considered it, and a fitting time was come, the King said to him, "Man of Athens, I have heard much of thee in time past, of thy wisdom and of thy journeyings to and fro, for they say that thou wanderest over many lands, seeking for knowledge. I have therefore a desire to ask of thee one question: 'Whom thinkest thou to be the happiest of all the men that thou hast seen?'" And this he said hoping that Solon would answer, "Thou, O King, art the happiest man that I have seen." But Solon flattered him not a whit, but spake the truth, saying, "O King, the happiest man that I have seen was Tellus the Athenian." Then Crœsus, marvelling much at these words, said, "And why thinkest thou that Tellus the Athenian was the happiest of men?" Then Solon answered, "Tellus saw his country in great prosperity, and he had children born to him that were fair and noble, and to each of these also he saw children born, of whom there died not one. Thus did all things prosper with him in life, as we count prosperity, and the end of his days also was great and

3

glorious; for when the Athenians fought with certain neighbours of theirs in Eleusis, he came to the help of his countrymen against their enemies, and put these to flight, and so died with great honour; and the whole people of the Athenians buried him in the same place wherein he fell, and honoured him greatly."

But when Solon had ended speaking to the King of Tellus, how happy he was, the King asked him again, "Whom, then, hast thou seen that was next in happiness to this Tellus?" For he thought to himself, "Surely now he will give me the second place." Then Solon said, "I judge Cleobis and Biton to have been second in happiness to Tellus."

Cleobis and Biton were youths of the city of Argos. They had a livelihood such as sufficed them; and their strength was greater than that of other men. For not only did they win prizes of strength, but also they did this thing that shall now be told. The men of Argos held a feast to Heré, who hath a great and famous temple in their city; and it must needs be that the mother of the two young men, being priestess of Heré, should be drawn in a waggon from the city to the temple; but the oxen that should have drawn the waggon were not yet come from the fields. Then, as the time pressed and the matter was urgent, the young men harnessed themselves to the waggon and dragged it, and their mother the priestess sat upon it. And the space for which they dragged it was forty and five furlongs; and so they came to the temple. And when they had done this in the eyes of all the assembly, there befell them such a death that nothing could be more to be desired;

4

the Gods, indeed, making it manifest that it is far better for a man to die than to live. For indeed the thing fell out thus. When all the people of Argos came about the woman and her sons, and the men praised the youths for their great strength, and the women praised the mother that she had borne such noble sons, the mother in the joy of her heart stood before the image and prayed that the goddess would give to her sons, even Cleobis and Biton, that which the Gods judge it best for a man to have. And when the priestess had so prayed, and the young men had offered sacrifice, and made merry with their companions, they lay down to sleep in the temple, and woke not again, but so ended their days. And the men of Argos commanded the artificers that they should make statues of the young men, and these they offered to the god at Delphi.

But when Solon thus gave the second place of happiness to these young men, King Crœsus was very wroth, and said, "Man of Athens, thou countest my happiness as nothing worth, not deeming me fit to be compared even with common men." Then Solon made answer, "O Crœsus, thou askest me about mortal life to say whether it be happy or no, but I know that the Gods are jealous and apt to bring trouble upon men. I know also that if a man's years be prolonged he shall see many things that he would fain not see, aye, and suffer many things also. Now I reckon that the years of a man's life are threescore and ten, and that in these years there are twenty and five thousand days and two hundred. For this is the number, if a man reckon not the intercalated month. But if he reckon this, seeing that in threescore and ten years are thirty and five such months, and the days of these months are one thousand and fifty, then the whole sum of the days of a man's life is twenty and six thousand two hundred and fifty. Now of these days, being so many, not one bringeth to a man things like to those which another hath brought. Wherefore, O King, the whole life of man is full of chance. I see indeed that thou hast exceeding great wealth and art king of many men. But as to that which thou askest of me, I call thee not happy, till I shall know that thou hast ended thy days prosperously. For the man that hath exceeding great riches is in no wise happier than he that hath sufficient only for the day, unless good fortune also remain with him, and give him all things that are to be desired, even unto the end of his days. For many men that are wealthy beyond measure are nevertheless unhappy, and many that have neither poverty nor riches have yet great happiness, and he that is exceeding rich and unhappy withal, excelleth him that hath moderate possessions with happiness in two things only, but the other excelleth in many things. For the first hath the more strength to satisfy the desires of his soul, and also to bear up against any misfortune that cometh upon him; but the second hath not this strength; and indeed he needeth it not, for his good fortune keepeth such things far from him. Also he is whole in body, and of good health, neither doth misfortune trouble him, and he hath good children, and is fair to look upon. And if, over and above these things, he also end his life well, then I judge him to be the happy man whom thou seekest. But till he die, so long do I hold my judgment, and call him not happy indeed, but fortunate. It is impossible also that any man should comprehend in his life all things that be good. For even as a country sufficeth not for itself nor produceth all things, but hath certain things of its own and receiveth certain from others, and as that country which produceth the most is counted the best, even so is it with men, for no man's body sufficeth for all things, but hath one thing and lacketh another. Whosoever, O King, keepeth ever the greatest store of things, and so endeth his life in a seemly fashion, this man deserveth in my judgment to be called happy. But we must needs regard the end of all things, how they shall turn out; for the Gods give to many men some earnest of happiness, but yet in the end overthrow them utterly.

These were the words of Solon. But they pleased not King Crœsus by any means. Therefore the King made no account of him, and dismissed him as being a foolish and ignorant person, seeing that he took no heed of the blessings that men have in their hands, bidding them always have regard unto their end.

Now it came to pass after Solon had departed from Sardis that there came great wrath from the Gods upon King Crœsus, and this, doubtless, because he judged himself to be the happiest of all men. And it happened in this wise. He saw a vision in his sleep, that told him of the trouble that should come upon him with respect to his son. For the King had two sons; but the one was afflicted of the Gods, being dumb from his birth, but the other far surpassed his equals of age in all things. And the name of this son was Atys. Now the vision that he saw in his sleep showed him that Atys should be smitten with a spear-point of iron, and so die. Therefore when he woke from his sleep and considered the matter, being much terrified by the dream, he sought how he might best keep his son from this peril. First, then, he married him to a wife; and next, he suffered him not to go forth any more to battle, though he had been wont aforetime to be the captain of the host; and, besides all this, he took away all javelins and spears, and such like things that men are wont to use in battle, from the chambers of the men, and stored them elsewhere, lest perchance one of them should fall from its place where it hung upon the wall and give the youth a hurt.

Now it chanced that while the matter of the young man's marriage was in hand, there came to Sardis a certain stranger, upon whom there had come the great trouble of blood-guiltiness. The man was a Phrygian by birth, and of the royal house: and he came into the palace of Crœsus, after the custom of that country, and sought for one that should cleanse him from his guilt; and Crœsus cleansed him. (Now the manner of cleansing is the same, for the most part, among the Lydians as it is among the Greeks.) And when the King had done for him according to all that was prescribed in the law, he would fain know who he was, and whence he had come. Wherefore, he asked him, saying, "My friend, who art thou? and from what city of Phrygia—for that thou art a Phrygian I know—art thou come, taking sanctuary at my hearth? And what man or woman didst thou slay?" And the man answered, "O King, I am the son of Gordias, the son of Midas, and my name is Adrastus, and I slew my own brother, not wittingly. For this cause am I come to thee, for my father drave me out from my home, and I am utterly bereft of all things." To this King Crœsus made reply, "Thou art the son of friends, and to a friend art thou come. Verily as long as thou abidest here thou shalt lack for nothing that I can give thee. And as for thy trouble, it will be best for thee to bear it as easily as may be." So the man lived thenceforth in the King's palace.

Now about this time there was a mighty wild boar in Olympus, that is a mountain of Mysia. It had its den in the mountain, and going out thence did much damage to the possessions of the Mysians; and the Mysians had often sought to slay him, but harmed him not at all, but rather received harm themselves. At the last they sent messengers to the King; who stood before him, and said, "O King, a mighty monster of a wild boar hath his abode in our country and destroyeth our possessions, and though we would fain kill him we cannot. Now therefore we pray thee that thou wilt send thy son, and chosen youths with him, and dogs for hunting, that they may go with us, and that we may drive this great beast out of our land." But when they made this request Crœsus remembered the dream which he had dreamed, and said, "As to my son, talk no more about him, for I will by no means let him go, seeing that the youth is newly married to a wife, and careth now for other things. But chosen youths of the Lydians shall go with you, and all the hunting dogs that I have; and I will bid them do their utmost to help you, that ye may drive this wild beast out of your land." This was the King's answer;

and the Mysians were fain to be content with it. But in the meanwhile the youth came in, for he had heard what the Mysians demanded of his father; and he spake to the King, saying, "O my father, I was wont aforetime to win for myself great credit and honour going forth to battle and to hunting. But now thou forbiddest me both the one and the other, not having seen any cowardice in me or lack of spirit. Tell me, my father, what countenance can I show to my fellows when I go to the market, or when I come from thence? What manner of man do I seem to be to my countrymen? and what manner of man to the wife that I have newly married? What thinketh she of her husband? Let me therefore go to this hunting, or, if not, prove to me that it is better for me to live as I am living this day." To this Crœsus made answer, "My son, I have seen no cowardice or baseness or any such thing in thee; but there appeared to me a vision in my sleep, and it stood over me and said that thy days should be few, for that thou shouldest die being smitten by a spear-point of iron. For this reason I made this marriage for thee, and send thee not forth on such occasions as I was wont to send thee on, keeping thee under guard, if so be that I may shield thee from thy fate at the least so long as I shall live. For thou art now my only son, for of him whom the Gods have afflicted, making him dumb, I take no count." To this the young man made answer, "Thou hast good reason, my father, to keep guard over me, seeing that thou hast had such a dream concerning me; yet I will tell thee a thing that thou hast not understood nor comprehended in the dream. Thou sayest that the vision told thee that

I should perish by a spear-point of iron. Consider now, therefore, what hands hath a wild boar and what spear-point of iron, that thou shouldest fear for me? For if indeed the vision had said that I should perish by a tooth, or by any other thing that is like to a tooth, then thou mightest well do what thou doest; but seeing that it spake of a spear-point, not so. Now, therefore, that we have not to do battle with men, but with beasts, I pray thee that thou let me go." Then said King Crœsus, "It is well said, my son; as to the dream, thou hast persuaded me. Therefore I have changed my purpose, and suffer thee to go to this hunting." When he had said this, he sent for Adrastus the Phrygian; and when the man was come into his presence, he spake, saying, "Adrastus, I took thee when thou wast afflicted with a grievous trouble, though indeed with this I upbraid thee not, and I cleansed thee from thy guilt, and received thee into my palace, and sustained thee without any cost of thine. Now, therefore, it is well that thou shouldest make me some return for all these benefits. I would make thee keeper of my son now that he goeth forth to this hunting, if it should chance that any robbers or such folk should be found on the way to do him hurt. Moreover, it becometh thee, for thine own sake, to go on an errand from which thou mayest win renown; for thou art of a royal house and art besides valiant and strong." To this Adrastus made answer, "O King, I had not indeed gone to this sport but for thy words. For he to whom such trouble hath come as hath come to me should not company with happy men; nor indeed hath he the will to do it. But now, as thou art earnest in this matter, I must needs yield to thy request. Therefore I am ready to do as thou wilt; be sure, therefore, that I will deliver thee thy son, whom thou biddest me keep, safe and unhurt, so far as his keeper may so do." So the young men departed, and chosen youths with them, and dogs for hunting. And when they were come to the mountain of Olympus they searched for the wild boar, and when they had found it, they stood in a circle about it, and threw their spears at it. And so it fell out that this stranger, the same that had been cleansed from the guilt of manslaying, whose name was Adrastus, throwing his spear at the wild boar and missing his aim, smote the son of Crœsus. And the youth died of the wound, so that the vision of the King was fulfilled, that he should die by a spear-point. And straightway there ran one to tell the thing to Crœsus. And when he had come to Sardis, he told the King how they had fought with the wild boar, and how his son had died.

Crœsus was very grievously troubled by the death of his son; and this the more because he had been slain by the man whom he had himself cleansed from the guilt of blood. And in his great grief he cried out very vehemently against the Gods, and specially against Zeus, the god of cleansing, seeing that he had cleansed this stranger, and now suffered grievous wrong at his hands. He reproached him also as the god of hospitality and of friendship—of hospitality, because he had entertained this man, and knew not that he was entertaining the slayer of his own son; and of friendship, because he had sent him to be a keeper and friend to his son, yet had found him to be an enemy and destroyer. And when he had done speaking there came Lydians bearing the dead body of the young man, and the slayer followed behind. So soon, therefore, as the man was come into the presence of the King, he gave himself up, stretching forth his hands, and bidding the King slay him on the dead body. And he spake of the dreadful deed that he had done before, and that now he had added to it a worse thing, bringing destruction on him that had cleansed him; and he cried out that he was not fit to live. But when Crœsus heard him speak, he pitied him, for all that he was in grievous trouble of his own, and spake to him, "I have had from thee, O my friend, all the vengeance that I need, seeing that thou hast pronounced sentence of death against thyself. But indeed thou art not the cause of this trouble, save only that thou hast brought it to pass unwittingly; some god is the cause, the same that long since foretold to me this very thing that hath now befallen me." So Crœsus buried his son with all due rites. But Adrastus the son of Gordias the son of Midas, that had been the slayer of his own brother, and had now slain the son of him that had cleansed him, waited behind till all men had left the sepulchre, and then slew himself upon it; for he knew that of all the men in the world he was the most unhappy.

CHAPTER II

CRŒSUS, WISHING TO MAKE WAR AGAINST THE PERSIANS, CONSULTETH THE ORACLES

FOR the space of two years did King Crœsus sit sorrowing for his son. But in the third year his thoughts were turned to other matters. For he heard that the kingdom of Astyages the son of Cyaxares had been overthrown by Cyrus the son of Cambyses, and that the power of the Persians increased day by day. For which reason it seemed good to him that he should prevent this people, if by any means he could, before they should become too mighty for him. And so soon as he had conceived this purpose in his heart, he made trial of all the oracles that are both in Europe and in Asia, sending messengers to Delphi, and to Abæ that belongeth to Phocis, and to Dodona. Also he sent to the oracles of Amphiaraüs, and of Trophonius, and of Branchidæ that is in Miletus. These are the oracles in the land of Greece of which he sent to enquire, and in Libya he sent to the oracle of Hammon. First he sent to make trial of all these whether they should be found to know the truth about a certain thing, purposing that if they should be so found he would send to them yet again and enquire whether he should take it in hand to make war against the Persians. Now he had given commandment to the messengers whom he sent to make trial of the oracles, that they should reckon the days diligently from the day whereon they set out from Sardis, and that on the hundredth day they should enquire of the oracles, saying, "What doth Crœsus the son of Alyattes, king of Lydia, chance to be doing this day?" and that they should write down the words of the oracle and bring them back to him. Now what the other oracles answered no man knows; but at Delphi, so soon as the Lydians were come into the temple to enquire of the god, the Pythia, for so they call the priestess that uttereth the mind of the god, spake, saying—

> "I know the number of the sand,
>   I know the measures of the sea;
> The dumb man's speech I understand,
>   Though nought he say, 'tis clear to me.
> I smell a savour new and sweet;
>   Strange is the feast the Lydians keep;
> Mingled in brazen caldron meet
>   The tortoise flesh and flesh of sheep;
> Around the burning embers glow,
>   With brass above and brass below."

These words the Lydians wrote down from the mouth of the Pythia, and so departed, and went their way to Sardis. The other messengers also came, bringing with them the oracles that had been delivered to them. Then the King opened each and read the writing; and not one of them pleased him. But when he knew the answer that had been brought from Delphi, forthwith he prayed and received it with reverence, for he judged that there was no true oracle in the world save that of Delphi only, seeing that it had discovered the very thing that he was doing. For after that he had sent his messengers to the oracles, when the appointed day was come, he devised this device. He imagined something that could not, he thought, by any means be discovered; for he chopped up together the flesh of a tortoise and the flesh of a lamb, and cooked them himself in a brazen caldron, upon which he had put a lid of brass. This was the answer that came to Crœsus from Delphi; but as to the oracle of Amphiaraüs, the answer that it made to the messengers when they had duly enquired of it no man knows, yet did Crœsus think that this also was a true oracle.

Here shall be told the story of Alcmæon of Athens, to whom Crœsus sent bidding him come to Sardis, for that he had helped the King's messengers when they enquired of the god at Delphi, furthering their business with all diligence. And when Alcmæon was come, the King said to him that he should be permitted to go into his treasury, and take therefrom for himself all the gold that he could carry on his body. Then Alcmæon prepared himself for this business. First he clothed himself with a tunic, in which he made a great fold for a pocket; and next he got him the widest and biggest boots that he could find, and so went into the treasury. And lighting on a heap of dust of gold he filled his boots with it as much as they would contain, even up to his knees; and also the fold of his tunic he filled with gold; also into his hair he put so much of the dust as it would contain. Other gold he took into his mouth, and so made his way out of the treasury, but scarcely could he drag his boots after him; and indeed he seemed like to anything rather than to a man, for his mouth was filled out and swollen beyond all a man's semblance. And when Crœsus saw him he laughed, and gave him all that gold and as much more. This was the beginning of the wealth of the house of Alcmæon.

After this King Crœsus sought to propitiate the god that was in Delphi with many and great sacrifices. For first he sacrificed three thousand beasts of all such as it is lawful to offer to the Gods, and next he builded up a great pile of couches that were covered with gold and silver, and of cups of gold, and of purple garments and tunics, and set fire to the pile, for he thought that by so doing he should make the god a friend to him. And he gave commandment to the Lydians that they should sacrifice in like manner every one of them such things as they had. And when this sacrifice was ended, he melted a great store of gold, and made bricks of it. Of these the bigger sort were six hand-breadths in length, and the smaller three hand-breadths, and all of them a hand-breadth in height. There were one hundred and sixteen of these bricks in all, four of them being of pure gold, and weighing each one talent and half a talent, and the rest of gold that was mixed with alloy; these weighed two talents to the brick. Also he made the image of a lion of pure gold, ten talents in weight. This lion, when the temple of Delphi was burnt, fell down from the bricks (for it had been set up on them);

and now it lieth in the treasury of the Corinthians, and weigheth seven talents and half a talent.

When Crœsus had finished casting these bricks, he sent them to Delphi and other things with them; to wit, two very great mixing bowls, of gold the one, and of silver the other. The bowl of gold lieth now in the treasury of the Corinthians, being in weight four talents and half a talent and twelve ounces. And the silver bowl lieth in the corner of the ante-chamber. It holdeth six hundred firkins; and the Delphians mix wine in it at the feast of the Showing of the Images. Also he sent four silver casks, that stand now in the treasury of the Corinthians, and two vessels for sprinkling water, of gold the one and of silver the other. On the gold bowl are written these words: "This the Lacedæmonians offered to the god." But these words are not true, for a certain man of Delphi (whose name, though it be known, shall not be mentioned in this place) engraved them, thinking to please the Lacedæmonians. Yet the boy, through whose hand the water flows, is an offering of the Lacedæmonians, but of the vessels themselves neither the one nor the other. Other offerings of no great account did Crœsus send to Delphi. Yet of one must mention be made; to wit, the golden statue of a woman three cubits in height. This the men of Delphi affirm to be the likeness of the bread-cutter of King Crœsus. Also the King offered to the god the necklace of his wife and her girdles also. He sent gifts likewise to the temple of Amphiaraüs.

Now Crœsus gave commandment to the Lydians that carried these offerings for him to Delphi and to the temple of Amphiaraüs, that they should enquire of the oracles whether or no he should make war against the Persians, and whether he should seek to gain for himself any allies that should help him. So when the Lydians that had been sent on this errand were come, they enquired of the oracles, saying, "Crœsus, king of the Lydians, and of other nations, holding these to be the only truth-speaking oracles that are among men, sendeth to you gifts that are worthy of your wisdom, and would now enquire of you whether he shall make war against the Persians, and also in what nations he shall seek for allies for himself." These are the things that the messengers of Crœsus enquired of the oracles, and the two agreed together in their answers; for first they said, "If Crœsus make war against the Persians, he shall bring to the ground a great empire," and next they counselled him to find out who of the Greeks were the most powerful at that season, and to make them his allies. This answer rejoiced the King exceedingly, for he made sure that he should bring the empire of Cyrus and the Persians to the ground. Wherefore he sent again to Delphi, and gave to every man two gold pieces, having first enquired how many men there were in the city; for which bounty the people of Delphi gave ill return to him and all other Lydians that they should have first approach to the oracle, and should be free of tribute, and should have the chief seat at feasts and games. Also that any man of Lydia might, if he so willed, be free of the city of Delphi.

After he had bestowed this bounty on the men of Delphi, Crœsus enquired of the oracle the third time; for now that he had assured himself that it spake the truth, he was instant in using of it. Therefore he enquired of it again; and this time he would fain know whether his kingdom should remain for many years. To this the oracle answered these words—

"Man of Lydia, when the mule
O'er the Medians' land shall rule,
Think of name and fame no more,
Fly by Hermus' stony shore."

And Crœsus, when he heard these words, was yet more exceedingly delighted, for he said to himself, "Surely now a mule shall never be king of the Medes in the place of a man. Wherefore this kingdom shall abide to me and my children after me for ever." After this he enquired what city of the Greeks was the most powerful at that season; and he found that there were two cities excelling in strength; to wit, Athens and Sparta, but that of these the city of Athens was much troubled by strife within itself, but that Sparta was prosperous exceedingly, and had of late years subdued unto itself the greater part of the island of Pelops, in which island it is. For these causes he sent messengers to Sparta with gifts, who spake after this manner, "Crœsus, king of Lydia and of other nations, hath sent us, saying, 'Men of Lacedæmon, the god, even Apollo, hath commanded me that I should make to myself friends of the Greeks, whomsoever I should find to be the strongest. Now, therefore, seeing that I find you to be the chiefest people in Greece, I do the bidding of the oracle, and come to you, and would have you for my friends and allies in all honesty and good faith.' " These words King Crœsus spake by the mouth of his messengers. And the thing pleased the Lacedæmonians well, for they also had heard the words of the oracle; and they made a treaty with Crœsus, and confirmed their friendship and alliance with an oath. And indeed there had been certain kindnesses done to their city by King Crœsus aforetime. For they had sent messengers to Sardis to buy gold for a certain statue that they would make; but when they sought to buy it, Crœsus gave it to them for a gift. For this cause the Lacedæmonians made alliance with Crœsus; also they were well pleased that he had chosen them out of all the Greeks to be his friends. So they made themselves ready to help him when he should call upon them; and they prepared a mixing bowl of brass, wrought on the outside of it with divers figures of beasts about the brim. This bowl held three hundred firkins; and the Lacedæmonians thought fit to give it to Crœsus in return for the things that he had given to them. Now the bowl came never to Sardis; but as to why it came not some say one thing and some say another. The Lacedæmonians say indeed that when the men that had charge of it were near to the island of Samos, the Samians came forth with ships of war, and assailed them, and took away the bowl from them. But the men of Samos say that they who had charge of it, when they found that the time had passed, Sardis being now taken by Cyrus, sold the bowl in Samos, and that certain persons bought it and offered it for an offering in the temple of Heré. Perchance the truth of the matter is this, that the men sold it indeed, yet affirmed when they were returned to Sparta that the Samians had taken it by force. And this is the story of the bowl.

After these things Crœsus marched with a great army into the land of Cappadocia, not reading the oracle aright, but hoping that he should bring to the ground the power of Cyrus and the Persians. And while he was yet making preparations for war there came to him a certain man of Lydia whose name was Sandanis. The man had been before accounted wise, but thenceforth had such renown for wisdom among the Lydians as had none beside. The man spake thus, "O King, the men against whom thou art preparing to make war have tunics of leather, and all their other garments also are of leather, and for food they have not what they would but what they can get, and the country wherein they dwell is rocky and barren. Also they use not wine, but drink water only; nor have they figs to eat, nor indeed any good thing, If therefore, O King, thou shalt conquer these men, what wilt thou take from them, for indeed they have nothing. But if they should prevail over thee, think what good things thou wilt lose. For when they have once tasted our good things they will hold fast by them, nor wilt thou drive them away. As for me, I thank the Gods that they have not put it into the hearts of the Persians to march against the land of Lydia." For it was so that the Persians before they conquered the Lydians had no good things of their own. For all that Sandanis prevailed not with King Crœsus to turn him from his purpose.

CHAPTER III

KING CRŒSUS IS DEFEATED AND THE CITY OF SARDIS IS TAKEN

KING CRŒSUS, being steadfastly purposed to make war with the Persians, marched into the land of the Cappadocians, wherein is the river Halys, being the boundary between his kingdom and the kingdom of Cyrus. Now the reasons that King Crœsus had for making war were these. First, he desired to enlarge the borders of his dominion, adding thereto the land of the Persians; and next, he had it in his heart to avenge upon Cyrus his sister's husband Astyages; for Cyrus had subdued him, and taken from him his kingdom, as shall be told hereafter. But how it came to pass that Crœsus was brother-in-law to Astyages shall be told at this present. Certain families of the wandering Scythians, being at variance with their own people, fled into the land of the Medes, the king of the Medes in those days being Cyaxares, the son of Phraortes. This Cyaxares at the first dealt kindly with these Scythians, as being men who were suppliants for his grace. And indeed he made so much of them that he put with them certain children who should learn their language and the art of shooting with the bow, in which they excel. Now the Scythians were wont to go hunting every day, and failed not to bring home venison; but after a while, on a certain day it chanced that they brought home nothing. And when King Cyaxares saw them returning with empty hands he was wroth with them, and entreated them shamefully, being indeed a man of violent temper. Then the Scythians bethought them how they might avenge themselves for this dishonour; whereupon they took one of the children whom they were teaching, and cut him into pieces, and dressed the flesh as they were wont to dress the venison which they took in hunting, and gave it to the King as if it were some wild beast which they had slain. But so soon as they had given it they fled to Alyattes at Sardis; and Cyaxares and his guests eat of the meat which had been prepared in this fashion. Now when the King heard how the Scythians had dealt with him, he sent to Alyattes and demanded that they should be given over to him for punishment, but Alyattes would not. After this there was war between the Lydians and the Medes for five years; and in this war the Lydians oftentimes had the advantage, and the Medes also oftentimes. But when they had fought against each other with equal fortune for five years, it so befell that in the sixth year, when they joined battle for the first time, the day became dark as the night. And this change of day into night Thales of Miletus had foretold, and indeed had appointed for it the selfsame year wherein it happened. But when the Lydians and the Medes saw what had befallen, they were the more eager to make peace the one with the other; and they that brought about this agreement were Syennesis of Cilicia, and Labynetus of Babylon. These caused that the two kings should make a treaty the one with the other, and should confirm it with an oath. Moreover, they made a covenant that Alyattes should give his daughter Aryenis to the son of Cyaxares to wife, and this son was Astyages; for they knew that such treaties stand not firm without there be some bond by which they that make them are bound. As for these nations they make oaths in the same fashion as do the Greeks; only they add this, that they make a cutting upon their arms, and they lick up the blood each man from the arm of the other.

When Crœsus with his army was come to the river Halys, he was in great doubt how he should cross it. But Thales of Miletus, who chanced to be in the camp of the King, contrived a device by which it was done. For he caused that the river, which before had flowed on the left hand of the army, should flow upon the right hand. And this he did by digging a deep ditch into which the river was turned before it came to the place where the army was encamped; and this, being made of the shape of a crescent, was carried in the rear of the army, and so was brought again into the river. Thus was the stream of the Halys divided between the river and the ditch; and being divided it could easily be crossed. Some stories say that the river was wholly dried up, all the water flowing into the ditch. But this is altogether incredible, for if the whole river had been turned into the ditch, how could King Crœsus with his army have crossed it when he returned from the battle with Cyrus to Sardis? And indeed it is scarcely to be believed that the river was so turned, though this story be commonly told among the Greeks, who say that there were no bridges over the Halys in those days, but rather it is to be believed that there were bridges, and that the King led his army across by them.

When Crœsus had crossed the Halys he came to a city of Cappadocia that was called Pterium; and this Pterium was the biggest and strongest city of those parts, lying as near as may be over against Sinope, which is on the Black Sea. This city Crœsus took by assault, and sold all the dwellers therein for slaves, and took also all the towns thereof, and removed out of the place where they dwelt all the people, though indeed they had done him no wrong. When Cyrus heard that King Crœsus was come against him, he also gathered his army together and went to meet him, taking with him as many as dwelt on the way by which he marched. But before that he set out he sent out heralds to the Ionians, bidding them revolt from Crœsus, whom indeed they served unwillingly; but the Ionians would not hearken to him. Cyrus therefore came up and pitched his camp over against the camp of the Lydians, which was near to the city of Pterium; and after a while the two kings joined battle. And the battle waxed hot, and many were slain on both sides, but neither gained the advantage; and when it was night they separated perforce. But Crœsus was ill content with the number of his army, for it was less by many thousands than the army of Cyrus. For which reason on the next day, seeing that Cyrus came not forth from his camp to assail him, he departed with all haste, returning to Sardis, for he had it in his mind to call the Egyptians to his help, according to his covenant with them, for he had made alliance with Amasis king of Egypt before he made alliance with the Lacedæmonians. Also he would send for help to the men of Babylon, for with these also he had alliance; and in those days Labynetus was king of Babylon. Lastly he sent a summons to the Lacedæmonians that they should send an army to him at the appointed time. For his purpose was that he should gather together all these his allies, and should also collect as great an army as might be of his own people, and so, when the winter was past, and the spring was come again, should march against the Persians. Having therefore these thoughts in his heart, so soon as he came to Sardis he sent heralds to Babylon, and to Egypt, and to Sparta, saying that they should send each of them an army to him at Sardis in the fifth month from that time; but as for the soldiers that he had hired with money, these he sent away, suffering them to be altogether scattered, for it did not so much as enter his thoughts that Cyrus, seeing that he had not done more than fight with him on equal terms, would march against Sardis. Now while he was busy considering these things there befell this marvel, that the whole space before the city was filled with serpents, and that so soon as the serpents were seen there the horses, leaving their accustomed pasture, fell to and devoured them. This thing Crœsus held to be a portent, as indeed it was; and straightway he sent messengers to Telmessus, where there are those that interpret such things. But these messengers, though indeed they went to Telmessus and heard from the interpreters what the meaning of this portent might be, were not able to show the matter to the King; for before that they came back to Sardis King Crœsus had been vanquished and taken prisoner. But the meaning of the portent according to the interpreters of Telmessus was this, "Let Crœsus look to see an army of strangers in his land; and let him know that when this army is come to his land it will subdue the inhabitants thereof; for the serpent is a son of the land, but the horse is a stranger and an enemy." This was the answer of the interpreters of Telmessus; and they made it when Crœsus was already vanquished, but they knew nothing of that which had befallen Sardis and the king thereof.

SCULPTURES FROM PTERIUM, A CITY DESTROYED
BY CRŒSUS.

But so soon as Crœsus had departed after the battle at Pterium, Cyrus, knowing that he had it in his thought to scatter his army, judged that he should do well if he marched straightway against Sardis before that the Lydians could gather themselves together against him a second time. And this thing he did without delay. For he marched into the land of Lydia with all haste; nor did Crœsus receive any message of his coming before that he saw the King himself with his army. Then was Crœsus sorely perplexed, for the matter had turned out wholly against his expectations. Nevertheless he took heart and led out the Lydians to battle. And indeed in those days there was not in the whole land of Asia any nation that was more stalwart and valiant than the nation of the Lydians. The people were accustomed to fight from horseback, carrying long spears, nor were there any horsemen more skilful. The Lydians therefore and the Persians were arrayed one against the other in the plain that lieth before Sardis, and this plain is very great and wholly bare of trees. But when Cyrus saw the array of the Lydians he was afraid of their horsemen, so many and well equipped were they. Then a certain Mede, Harpagus by name, counselled him what he should do, and Cyrus hearkened to him. He took all the camels that followed his army, carrying victuals and baggage, and taking their burdens from them, set riders upon them, arming all of them as horsemen. And having so furnished the camels, he commanded that they should go before his army against the horsemen of Crœsus. And behind the camels he put the foot soldiers, and behind the foot soldiers the horsemen. And when the whole army was drawn up in battle array, he straightway commanded them that they should slay all else of the Lydians, who might fall in their way, but that Crœsus himself they should not slay, not even if he should defend himself when they laid hands upon him. Now the reason why he set the camels in array against the horsemen was this. The horse is sore afraid of the camel, and cannot endure to look upon the shape of the beast or to smell the smell. For this cause therefore he used this device, that the King of the Lydians might find no gain from his horsemen, by whom he hoped that he should win a great victory. And indeed so soon as ever the two armies had joined battle, and the horses smelled the smell of the camels and saw them, they turned and fled. So was Crœsus utterly disappointed of his hope. Nevertheless the Lydians bare themselves bravely; for when they saw what had befallen them, they leapt from their horses and fought with the Persians on foot. But after a while, when many had been slain on both sides, the Lydians were driven into their city, and were besieged therein by the Persians.

Now it seemed to Crœsus that the siege would be of many months. Therefore he sent again other messengers to his allies saying that, whereas he had before bidden them to assemble themselves at Sardis in the fifth month, there was now need that they should come with all the speed that might be, for that the King was besieged. Now of the other allies nothing need be said; but as to the Lacedæmonians, when the messengers of Crœsus came to them, they were at variance with their neighbours, the men of Argos. Notwithstanding, they made all haste to come to the help of the King; and were indeed ready to set forth, with ships duly furnished, when there came to them tidings that the city of Sardis was taken and Crœsus led into captivity. When they heard this they changed their purpose and went not; nevertheless they thought it a grievous thing.

Now the taking of Sardis was in this wise. On the fourteenth day after the beginning of the siege, Cyrus sent horsemen throughout his army, saying that he would give great gifts to the man who should first mount upon the wall. But when the whole army had attacked the city, and prevailed nothing, a certain Mardian, whose name was Hyrœades, desisted not as did the others, but made his attempt on a certain part of the citadel where no sentinels were set. And none were set because no man had any fear that the citadel could be taken from this quarter, for the place was very steep. And this indeed was the only part of the citadel to which Meles, who had been king of Sardis in old time, had not caused the lion's cub to be carried. Now the story of the lion's cub is this. A woman in Sardis brought forth a young lion, and the interpreters of Telmessus said, "If thou carry the young lion round about its wall, no man shall take Sardis." So Meles caused them to carry the cub round about the wall wherever it could be attacked, but of this place he took no account, so steep was it and hard of access. Now Hyrœades had seen on the day before that a certain Lydian had come down by this place after a helmet that had rolled down from the top, and had fetched the helmet, and so returned. And having seen this thing he bare it in mind; and the next day he climbed up the same way, and many Persians after him. So Sardis was taken and all the city plundered. As to the King himself, there befell this thing that shall now be told. He had a son, of whom indeed mention has been made before. A goodly youth he was in all other respects, but he was dumb. Now in the days of his prosperity Crœsus, having done many other things that the youth might be healed of his infirmity, sent also messengers to the oracle of Delphi to enquire of the god. To these the Pythia made answer in these words—

> "O king of many lands, the thought
>   Thou keepest in thy heart is vain:
> The help with many prayers besought
>   Think not to ask of heaven again;
> For ill the day and full of fear
> That first thy dumb child's voice shall hear."

Now it came to pass that when the Persians were taking the citadel, one of them made as if he would have slain Crœsus, not knowing who he was. And Crœsus, though he saw the man coming against him, heeded him not, so great was his trouble; for he thought that it would be well for him to die. But the youth, that had been dumb all his days, when he saw the Persian about to strike, by reason of his fear and of the instant necessity of the thing, cried out, saying, "Fellow, slay not King Crœsus." Thus did he speak for the first time; but afterwards, for the rest of his life, he spake even as other men.

CHAPTER IV

CRŒSUS IS SAVED FROM DEATH. OF LYDIA, THE LYDIANS, AND OF CERTAIN GREEKS THAT DWELT IN ASIA

So the Persians gained possession of the city of Sardis. And Crœsus himself they took alive, and led him to Cyrus their king; and all the years that he had reigned were fourteen; fourteen also was the number of the days for which his city was besieged. And thus was the prophecy of the oracle fulfilled, that he should bring to an end a great empire; to wit, his own. Then Cyrus commanded that they should build a great pile of wood, and should set Crœsus thereon bound in chains, and with him fourteen men of Lydia, and burn them with fire. But whether in so doing he thought to offer the first-fruits of his victory to some god, or was performing a vow which he had made, or having heard that Crœsus had been a great worshipper of the Gods, desired now to see whether any god would come and help him in his need, cannot certainly be known. But when Crœsus stood upon the pile, and the fire had now been put to it, there came into his thoughts, notwithstanding the great strait wherein he stood, that the saying of Solon was indeed true, and spoken by inspiration of the Gods, when he said that none of living men might be counted happy. And when he thought of this he cried out with a loud voice, having before kept silence altogether, "Solon, Solon, Solon!" which when Cyrus heard, he bade the interpreters ask of Crœsus who was this that he called upon. But when the interpreters asked this thing, for a time Crœsus kept silence, but afterwards, for indeed he was constrained to speak, made this answer, "He is one with whom it would be better than many possessions for all rulers to have speech." Then, as no man could understand these words, they enquired of him again what they might signify. And as they were earnest with him, and would not leave him in peace, he told them how there had come to his court one Solon, a man of Athens, who having seen all his wealth and prosperity, had made little account of it; and how that there had befallen him all that this same Solon had said, though indeed the man spake not of him in particular but of all mortal men, and especially of those who judged themselves to be happy. This was the answer which Crœsus made; and now the pile had been lighted, and the extremities were on fire. But when Cyrus heard from the interpreters the words of Crœsus, he repented him of his purpose, bethinking him how that he, being but a mortal man, was now giving another man that had aforetime been not less prosperous than himself to be burned with fire, and fearing lest there should come upon him vengeance for such a deed, and considering also that there was nothing sure in human affairs. For which reasons he bade them that stood by quench the fire and cause Crœsus and the men that were with him to descend from the pile. But these, with all their striving, could not prevail over the fire. Then Crœsus—for this is the story of the Lydians—when he saw that Cyrus had repented him of his purpose, and that every one was striving to quench the fire but could not, cried with a loud voice to Apollo, beseeching the god that if he had ever made an offering that was to his liking, he would deliver him from his present peril. This he besought of the god with many tears, and lo! of a sudden, though the day before had been fine and calm, there came a great storm with a most vehement rain, which quenched the fire. Then Cyrus knew of a surety that Crœsus was a good man and dear to the Gods. And having caused him to descend from the pile, he asked him, saying, "Tell me, Crœsus, what man persuaded thee to lead thy army against my land, and to make me thine enemy, having been before thy friend?" Then Crœsus answered, "This I did, O King, for thy good fortune, but to my loss. Nor was it a man that did this, but the god of the Greeks, who encouraged me to make war against thee. For surely no man is so foolish that of his own will he should choose war instead of peace; for in peace the children bury their fathers, but in war the fathers bury their children. But these things have fallen out as the Gods would have them." When he had said these things Cyrus bade them loose his chains, and put him near to himself, and marvelled when he regarded him, both he and the Persians that were with him. And Crœsus said nothing, thinking about many

CRŒSUS ON THE FUNERAL PILE

things. But after a while, when he saw the Persians plundering the city of the Lydians, he turned him to King Cyrus, and said, "Is it allowed to me, O King, to speak that which is in my heart, or shall I be silent?" And Cyrus bade him be of courage and speak what he would. Then Crœsus asked him, "What is it that this great multitude is so busy about?" "They are spoiling thy city," said Cyrus, "and carrying off thy possessions." "Nay," said Crœsus, "this is not my city that they spoil, nor my possessions that they carry off; for I have now no share or lot in these things. But the things that they plunder are thine." Then Cyrus took heed of the words which Crœsus had spoken to him; and bidding all others leave him, he asked him again what he thought of these matters. Then Crœsus made answer, "The Gods have made me thy servant; wherefore I count it right to tell thee if I perceive aught that thou seest not. The Persians are haughty by nature, but they are poor. And if thou sufferest them to plunder in this fashion and to gain for themselves great wealth, be sure that this will befall thee. That man among them who shall get the most will be he that will rebel against thee. If therefore my words please thee, do according to my bidding. Set spearmen as guards at all the gates, and let them take away from all that come out the things that they carry with them, saying at the same time, 'We must needs give tithe to Zeus of all these things.' And they will not hate thee as if thou didst take the things from them by force, but will judge thee to do that which is right, and will give them up willingly." When Cyrus heard these words he was pleased with them beyond measure, judging them to have been wisely said. So when he had commended Crœsus for his wisdom, and had given commandment to the spearmen according to these words, he said, "Thou hast it in thy heart to do good deeds and to say good words as befitteth a king; ask therefore some boon of me which thou wouldest have granted to thee straightway." Then said Crœsus, "O King, thou canst not please me more, than if thou wilt suffer me to send to the god of the Greeks, whom I have honoured with gifts more than all Gods beside, and to lay these fetters before him, and ask him whether it is his custom to deceive them that do him honour." And when Cyrus would know why he desired to put this question accusing the god, Crœsus set before him the whole matter, both that which he had asked, and the answer of the god, and the offerings which he had made, and how he had made war against the Persians, being encouraged thereto by the god. And when he had ended this tale he besought Cyrus again that he would suffer him to reproach the god with these things. And Cyrus, when he heard it, laughed and said, "This request I grant thee, O Crœsus, as I will grant thee everything that thou shalt ask me hereafter." And when Crœsus heard these words he sent certain Lydians to Delphi, and bade them lay the fetters on the threshold of the temple and enquire of the god whether he was not ashamed to have encouraged Crœsus by his oracles to march against the Persians, thinking that he should overthrow the empire of Cyrus, of which undertaking these, the fetters to wit, were the first-fruits, and whether it was the custom of the god of the Greeks to be unfaithful. And when the

Lydians did as had been commanded them, the Pythia made this answer, "That which is fated it is by no means possible to avoid, not even to a god. And Crœsus hath suffered for the transgressions of his forefather in the fifth generation, who, being a body-guard of the king, slew his master, a woman helping him with her craft, and took his honour to himself, though he had no part or lot in it. And Apollo was very earnest with the Fates that they should not bring this evil upon Sardis in the days of Crœsus, but that they should bring it in his son's days. Yet could he not prevail. Nevertheless all that the Fates granted to him that did he for Crœsus, delaying the taking of Sardis for the space of three years; for let Crœsus be sure of this, that the taking of Sardis is later by three years than had been ordained at the first. Also when he was in peril of being burnt with fire the god helped him and delivered him. And as for the oracle, Crœsus doth not right to blame him, for Apollo foretold to him that, if he should make war against the Persians, he should bring to the ground a great empire. If therefore he had been well advised in this matter, he should have sent again to enquire of the god whether his own empire or the empire of Cyrus were thus signified. But seeing that he understood not the thing which was said, nor enquired a second time, let him blame himself. And as to that which Apollo answered him when he enquired of him the last time, speaking of a mule, this also Crœsus understood not. For Cyrus was this mule, being born of parents that were not of the same race, his mother also being of the more noble stock and his father of the worse. For she was a woman of the Medes and the daughter of King Astyages, and he was a Persian and no king, but a servant that married the daughter of his master." This was the answer that the priestess gave to the Lydians; and when Crœsus heard it he confessed that he had erred and not the god.

In this way did the empire of the Lydians come to an end. These Lydians were the first that found out the coining of gold and silver. Also they were the first traders. And they say of themselves that they first made the games at which they and the Greeks are used to play. Also they declare that in the days when these games were first made by them they colonized the land of Tyrsenia, which is in Italy. And their story of this matter is this. In the days of Atys the son of Manes there was a sore famine throughout the whole land of Lydia. And for a while the Lydians were instant in prayers to the Gods that they would help them; but, as the famine ceased not, they sought for remedies, contriving some one thing and some another. In those days they devised dice-playing and ball-playing and all other kinds of games that men use, save chess only, for this the Lydians say not that they devised. And their manner with the games was this. One day they would play continually, that they might not have any thought for food, and the next day they would leave off from their playing and eat. In this fashion they endured for the space of eighteen years. But as the evil abated not but rather grew worse, the King divided the people of Lydia into two parts, making them cast lots, that the one part should remain in the land, and the other part should go forth to some other country. And that part which drew the lot for remaining he took to himself, but that part which should go forth he gave to his son, whose name was Tyrsenus. These then went down to the seacoast, to Smyrna, and there built them ships, into which they put all things that they needed for a voyage, and so set sail, seeking for livelihood and a country wherein they might dwell; in which search, having passed by many lands, they came to the land of the Umbri, and there built for themselves cities, in the which they dwell to this day. Also they changed their name, calling themselves no more Lydians but Tyrsenians, after the name of the King's son, Tyrsenus, who had led them forth.

Now the men of Ionia and Æolia, so soon as they knew that the Lydians had been subdued by the Persians, sent messengers to Cyrus, saying that they would fain be his servants after the same manner in which they had been the servants of Crœsus. But when they had made their oration to him he spake to them for an answer this parable. "A certain flute-player, seeing fishes in the sea, played his flute to them, thinking that they would come forth from the sea on to the land at his playing. But when they would not do as he had hoped, he took a net, and cast it, and having encompassed therewith a great multitude of fishes, he drew it to the land. And when he saw them that they flapped their tails upon the ground, he said, 'Cease this dancing, for ye would not come out and dance upon the land when I piped to you.'" This said Cyrus because in the beginning of the war he had sent to these men bidding them rebel against Crœsus, and they would not, but now when they knew that he had gotten himself the victory, they were ready to be his servants. For this cause he was very wroth with them; and when the men of Ionia and Æolia heard his words, they knew that he purposed evil against them, and began to prepare themselves accordingly.

First they sent messengers to Sparta to ask for help; who, when they were come, chose Pythermus, a man of Phocæa, to speak for them. This Pythermus, having clad himself in purple, which he did that all the Spartans might come together to see him, stood up in the assembly, and told his business. But the Spartans consented not to help; only after that the messengers had departed they sent certain men in a ship of fifty oars, who should see for themselves how things were with Cyrus and the Ionians. The chief of these men, a certain Lacrines, went up to Sardis, and declared to Cyrus the pleasure of the Lacedæmonians, that he should not harm any city of the Greeks, for that they would not suffer it. But when Cyrus heard these words he enquired of certain Greeks that were with him, what manner of men and how many in number these Lacedæmonians might be that they laid such commands upon him. And when he heard he said to Lacrines, "I regard not at all the folk who have a set place in the midst of their city whither they assemble and forswear themselves and deceive each other. Surely, if it be well with me, all that the Ionians have suffered they shall suffer." Cyrus said this reproaching the Greeks because they have markets wherein they buy and sell, for the Persians use not to do any such thing.

After this Cyrus departed, and took Crœsus with

him; and over Sardis and the Lydians he made a certain Persian, named Tabalus, governor, but the charge of the gold he gave to Pactyas, a man of Lydia. But Pactyas took the gold, and having hired soldiers besieged Tabalus in the citadel of Sardis. When tidings of these things were brought to Cyrus as he journeyed eastward, he changed not his purpose, having weightier things in hand, but sent Mazares a Mede with a part of the army to deal with the Lydians and Ionians. Of whose coming when Pactyas heard he escaped from the citadel of Sardis and fled to Cumæ. Whereupon Mazares sent messengers to Cumæ, bidding the inhabitants deliver up the enemy of the King. But the men of Cumæ doubted what they should do, and sent messengers to enquire of the god in Branchidæ of Miletus; to whom the god answered that they should deliver up Pactyas. But when this answer was brought back, and the people were now ready to deliver him up, the thing pleased not one of the chief men, Aristodicus by name, who persuaded the men of Cumæ that they should send yet again and enquire of the god by the hand of other messengers. So they sent other messengers, among whom was Aristodicus himself. When they were come to the oracle, Aristodicus, being spokesman for the rest, spake, saying, "O King, there came to us a certain Pactyas, a man of Lydia, flying from the Persians, who were ready to put him to death. And now these Persians will have us deliver him to them. But we, though we fear them, are yet loath to deliver the man to death, and so are come asking thee what we should do." To this the god answered again that they should deliver him up. But when Aristodicus heard this he went about the temple taking the young birds out of their nests, for many birds had built therein. As he did this there came a voice out of the shrine, "What doest thou, thou wicked man, taking these that have sought sanctuary with me?" Then Aristodicus answered, "O King, thou indeed defendest them that seek sanctuary with thee, but thou biddest the men of Cumæ deliver up this suppliant. And the god answered, "Yea, I bade you do this thing, that so ye might perish utterly, and might not ask such ill questions of the god any more." When the men of Cumæ heard these words they neither were willing to deliver him up nor to keep him, and so be besieged. Therefore they sent him to Mitylene. But when they knew that the men of Mitylene were preparing to deliver him up for a reward, they sent a ship and took him to Chios; but the Chians delivered him up to the Persians, receiving for him a certain place called Atarnes, which is in Mysia, over against Lesbos. And to this day Atarnes is accursed, and the Chians use not any of its fruits for sacrifice.

After this Tabalus, having subdued certain cities of Ionia, died, and Cyrus sent Harpagus a Mede, of whom there is much to be said hereafter, to be captain in his room. And the first city which Harpagus made ready to attack was Phocæa. Now the men of Phocæa were mighty sailors, and were the first of the Greeks to make long voyages, visiting, besides other places, Tartessus, which is in Spain. Now in Tartessus they found a certain king, whose name was Arganthonius. He was a very old man of sixscore years, and he had reigned in Tartessus fourscore years. This Arganthonius dealt very kindly with the Phocæans, and when he knew that the power of the Medes waxed great in Asia, gave them much money that they might build them a wall; which wall indeed they built of great stones well fitted together. Now when Harpagus was come to Phocæa, he sent messengers bidding them submit themselves to Cyrus; and he said that it would suffice if they would throw down one battlement on their wall, and set apart one house in their city. But the men of Phocæa asked for one day that they might deliberate, and would have Harpagus take his army from before their city for so long. Then said Harpagus, "I know well what ye purpose to do, yet shall ye have the day." And he took his army from before the city. Then the Phocæans launched their ships, and put therein their wives and children and their goods, and all the images from the temples, and all the offerings, save such as were of brass or stone, or pictures; and having done this they sailed to Chios; and the Persians took Phocæa, being deserted of its inhabitants.

But the Phocæans would fain have bought certain islands of the people of Chios, but these would not sell them, fearing lest they should suffer in trading. Then they sailed to Cyrnus, where twenty years before they had built a city. But first they sailed back to Phocæa and slew the garrison which Harpagus had set there to keep it; and having slain the garrison, they threw an anvil of iron into the sea, and sware that they would not return to the city till they should see the anvil floating on the water. Yet, while they were voyaging to Cyrnus, half and more repented them of their purpose, and brake their oath, and went back to Phocæa, and dwelt there. But such as kept to their oath sailed to Cyrnus, where they dwelt for five years. But at the end of five years the Phœnicians and the men of Carthage made alliance and sailed against them, for they plundered all the neighbouring parts. Then was there a great battle, and the Phocæans prevailed, yet lost forty ships out of threescore. Then those that remained sailed to Rhegium in Italy, and built a city in those parts.

The men of Tios did as the Phocæans had done, for they put all that they had in ships, and departed, and dwelt in a city of Thrace called Abdera. But all the other Ionians on the mainland submitted themselves to Cyrus; and the islanders did likewise, fearing what might befall them.

After this Harpagus subdued the other nations that are in those parts, as the Carians and the Lycians and others. About these there is nothing worthy to be told, save about the Lycians of Xanthus only. For these first of all fought against the Persians before their city, and being vanquished for all their valour, for they were few fighting against many, and being shut up in their city, yet would not yield themselves. For first they gathered together in their citadel their wives and their children and their slaves and all their goods, and burnt them with fire. And having done this, they bound themselves with dreadful oaths, and fell upon the Persians, and died fighting all of them.

CHAPTER V

THE BIRTH AND BRINGING UP OF CYRUS

ASTYAGES king of the Medes had a daughter whose name was Mandané; and of this daughter, when she was but a child, he dreamed such a dream that he feared exceedingly what might happen to him and to his kingdom by reason of her. Therefore when she grew of age to be married, he gave her not to a man of her own race, but he gave her to a Persian, whose name was Cambyses. And this Cambyses was indeed of a noble house, but of a quiet and peaceable temper. Only because he was a Persian, Astyages held him to be of less account than a Mede, whether he were noble or no.

But in the first year of the marriage King Astyages dreamed another dream of his daughter, which made him yet more afraid than had the former dream. Therefore he sent for the woman, who was now about to bring forth her first-born child, and kept her in the palace, being minded to put to death that which should be born of her, for the interpreters of dreams had signified to him that the son of his daughter should be king in his stead. When therefore she bare Cyrus, for they gave this name to the child, Astyages called to him one Harpagus, who was of his kindred, and faithful to him beyond all other of the Medes, and who had also the care of his household. And when Harpagus was come to him, the King said, "Harpagus, see thou that in the matter which I shall now put in thy charge thou in no wise neglect my commandment, nor prefer others to me, and so in the end bring great sorrow on thyself. Now the matter is this. Thou shalt take this child that Mandané my daughter hath lately borne, and carry it to thy home, and there slay it; and afterwards thou shalt bury it in such fashion as thou wilt." To this Harpagus said, "O King, thou hast never perceived any transgression in thy servant in time past; and he will take good heed that he sin not against thee in time to come. And as for this matter of which thou speakest, if thou wilt have it so, it must needs be done." When Harpagus had said this, they gave him the child into his hands, the child being dressed as if for death and burial, and he took it and went to his home weeping. And when he was come thither he said to his wife all the words that King Astyages had said to him. Then the woman spake, saying, "What then art thou minded to do in this matter?" And he said, "Of a surety I shall not do as the King hath commanded me. For though he should be turned aside to folly, and be stricken with madness even more grievously than he is now stricken, yet why should I be the slayer of this child? And the causes wherefore I will not do this thing are many. For first he is of my own kindred, and next Astyages is an old man and hath no male offspring. If then when he shall die, his kingdom shall go to his daughter, whose child he biddeth me to slay, surely I shall stand in great peril. It must needs be that the child die; for how else shall I escape, but the slayer shall be one of the servants of Astyages, and not I or one of my own servants." When he had thus spoken, he sent a messenger straightway to one of the herdsmen of Astyages, knowing that the man dwelt in a place well fitted for the purpose, that is to say, a mountain abounding in wild beasts. The name of this herdsman was Mitradates, and his wife was a slavewoman, Spaco by name. As for the pastures where he pastured his herd, they lay under the mountains which are northwards from Egbatana, towards the Black Sea. For this region of the land of Media is covered with woods and mountains, but the country for the most part is a plain country. The herdsman therefore being thus called came with all speed. And when he was come, Harpagus said to him, "Astyages bids thee take this child and put him in some desert place among the mountains that he may speedily perish. And he bids me say that if thou slay him not, but in any way sufferest him to live, he will destroy thee most miserably. And I am appointed to see that this thing be done."

When the herdsman heard these words he took the child and went on his way to his home, and came to the stalls of the cattle. Now it chanced that his wife had been in travail all that day, and that she bare a child while the herdsman was at the city. And the two were much troubled each about the other; for the husband feared lest haply it should go ill with his wife in her travail, and the woman was afraid because Harpagus had sent for her husband in much haste, which thing he had not been wont to do. When therefore he had returned, the woman, seeing that he was come back speedily and beyond her hope, asked of him, saying, "Why did Harpagus send for thee in such haste?" Then the man made answer, "When I was come to the city I saw and heard such things as I would had never befallen my masters; for the whole house of Harpagus was full of weeping and wailing. And when I went into the house, being sore astonished at these things, I saw a child lying there and crying; and the child was adorned with gold and fine clothing. And Harpagus, so soon as he saw me, bade me take up the child with all haste and depart, and put it on such mountain as I knew to be most haunted by wild beasts. And he said that King Astyages had given commandment that this should be done. And he added many threats of what should befall me, if I should not do as he had bidden me. Wherefore I took the child, and carried it away, thinking that it was the child of some one in the household; for the truth, as it was, I could not have imagined, yet did I marvel to see that the child was adorned with gold and fine apparel, and also that there should be so great a mourning in the house of Harpagus. But as I went on my way, one of the servants of Harpagus, whom he had sent with me, recounted to me the whole matter, that this child was the son of Mandané the daughter of Astyages and Cambyses the son of Cyrus, and that Astyages had given commandment that it should be slain. This therefore is the child whom thou seest." And when the herdsman had said this he took away the covering, and showed the child to his wife. And when she saw the babe, that it was fair and well-favoured, she wept, and laid hold of her husband by his knees and besought him that he would not do this thing, putting forth the child to die. But the man answered that he could not by any means do otherwise, for that Harpagus would send those who would see whether the thing had been done or no, and that he should perish miserably if he should be found to have transgressed the commandment. Then the woman, seeing that she could not prevail with her husband, spake to him again, saying, "If then I cannot prevail with thee that thou shouldest not put forth the child, yet listen to me. If the men must needs see a child put forth, do thou this thing that I shall tell thee. I was delivered of a child this day, and the child was dead when it was born. Take therefore this dead child and put it forth, and let us rear this child of the daughter of Astyages as if it were our own. So thou wilt not be found to transgress the commands of thy masters, and we shall also have done well for ourselves. For indeed the dead child shall have a royal burial, and the living child shall not be slain." And here the woman seemed to her husband the herdsman to have spoken very wisely and seasonably, and he did according to her word. For the child that he had brought with him that he might cause him to die, this he gave to his wife to rear; and his own child, being dead already, he put into the basket wherein he had carried the other. With this he put all the ornaments wherewith the child had been adorned, and carried it to the most desolate place that he knew among the mountains, and there laid it forth. And on the third day after he had done this, he went again to the city, leaving his herds in the charge of one of them that were under him, and entering into the house of Harpagus, said he was ready to show the dead body of the child to any whom he might send. Wherefore Harpagus sent such of his own body-guard as he judged to be most faithful, and saw the thing, not himself indeed, but with their eyes, and afterwards buried the child that was the child of the herdsman. As for the child that had afterwards the name of Cyrus, the wife of the herdsman took him and reared him, but called him by some other name. When the boy was ten years old there befell a thing by which his birth was discovered. He was wont to play with other boys that were his equals in age, in the village wherein were the dwellings of the herdsman and his fellows. And the boys in their sport chose him, being, as was supposed, the herdsman's son, to be their king. And he, being thus chosen, gave to each his proper work, setting one to build houses, and others to be his body-guards, and one to be the "Eye of the King," and others to carry messages, to each his own work. Now one of the boys that played with him, being the son of one Artembares, a man of renown among the Medes, would not do the thing which Cyrus had commanded him. Wherefore Cyrus bade the other boys lay hold of him; and when these had done his bidding he corrected him for his fault with many and grievous stripes. But the boy, so soon as he was let go, thinking that he had suffered a grievous wrong, went in great wrath to the city and made complaint to his father of the things which he had suffered at the hands of Cyrus; only he spake not of Cyrus, for he bare not as yet that name, but of the herdsman's son. Then Artembares, being in a great rage, went straightway to King Astyages, taking with him his son, as one that had been shamefully entreated. And he said to the King, "See, O King, how we have been wronged by this slave who is the son of thy herdsman." And he showed him the lad's shoulders, where might be seen the marks of the stripes. When Astyages heard and saw these things he was ready to avenge the lad on him that had done these things, wishing to do honour to Artembares. Therefore he sent for the herdsman and the boy. And when they were both come before him, Astyages looked towards Cyrus, "How didst thou, being the son of this herdsman, dare to do such shameful things to the son of a man who is first of all them that stand before me?" To this Cyrus made answer, "My lord, all this that I did, I did with good cause; for the boys of the village, this also being one of them, in their play chose me to be their king, for I seemed to them to be the fittest for this honour. All the others indeed did the things which I commanded them; but this boy was disobedient and paid no heed to me; for which things he received punishment as was due. And if thou deemest it fit that I should suffer for so doing, lo, here I am!" When the lad spake in this fashion, Astyages, considering with himself the whole matter, knew him who he was. For the likeness of his countenance betrayed him; his speech also was more free than could be looked for in the son of a herdsman, and his age also agreed with the time of putting forth the child of his daughter. And being beyond measure astonished at these things, for a while he sat speechless; but at last, having scarcely come to himself, he said to Artembares, "Artembares, I will so deal with this matter that neither thou nor thy son shall blame me," for he would have the man go forth from his presence, that having the herdsman alone he might question him more closely concerning these matters.

Then the King sent Artembares away, and bade his servants take Cyrus with them into the house. Being therefore left alone with the herdsman, he enquired of him, saying, "Tell me whence didst thou receive this child, and who is he that gave him to thee?" Then said the herdsman, "Surely he is my son, and she that bare him is my wife, and is yet alive in my house." But the King answered, "Thou answerest not well for thyself; thou wilt bring thyself into great peril." And he bade his guards lay hold upon him. But the man, when he saw that he was being led away to the tormentors, said that he would tell the whole truth. And indeed he unfolded the story from the beginning, and neither changed nor concealed anything. And when he had ended, he was earnest in prayer to the King that he would have mercy upon him and pardon him.

As for the herdsman indeed, when he had thus told the truth, Astyages took little heed of him; but he had great wrath against Harpagus, and sent to him by his guards that he should come forthwith. And when he was come, the King said to him, "Harpagus, how didst thou slay the boy whom I delivered to thee that was born of my daughter?" And Harpagus, seeing that the herdsman stood before the King, sought not to hide the matter, for he judged that he should be easily convicted if he should speak that which was false. Therefore he said, "O King, when I took the child from thy hands, I considered with myself how I might best do thy pleasure, so that I might both be blameless before thee, and also free of blood-guiltiness as concerning thy daughter. And I did after this manner. I called this herdsman to me, and gave the child into his hands, telling him that thou hadst given commandment that it should be slain. Then I bade him take the child, and put it out in some desert place among the mountains, and watch by it till it should die. And at the same time I used to him all manner of threats, if he should not in all things fulfill my words. And when the man had done according to my bidding, I sent the most faithful of my servants, and having seen by their eyes that the child was dead, I buried him. This is the truth of the matter, O King, and in this manner the child died."

When Harpagus had ended this story, wherein he spake, as he thought, the whole truth, Astyages hid his anger in his heart, and related the whole matter as he had heard it from the herdsman; and when it was ended, he said, "The boy yet lives; and it is well; for indeed I have been much troubled, remembering what had been done to the child; nor did I count it a light matter that my daughter was displeased with me. Now, therefore, that the matter hath turned out so well, first send thine own son that he may be a companion to this boy, and next come and dine with me to-day, for I would have a feast of thanksgiving for this boy that was dead and is alive again." When Harpagus heard these words, he bowed himself down before the King, rejoicing beyond measure that his transgression had had so good an ending, and that he had been called to the feast of thanksgiving; and he went to his house. And being come, in the joy of his heart he told to his wife all that had befallen him. But the King, so soon as the son of Harpagus was come into the house, took him and slew him, and cut him limb from limb; and of the flesh he roasted some, and some he boiled; and so, having dressed it with much care, made it ready against the dinner. And when the hour of dinner was come, Harpagus and the other guests sat down to meat; and before Harpagus was set a dish of the flesh of his own son, wherein was every part, save only the head and the tips of the hands and of the feet. For these lay apart by themselves with a covering over them. And when Harpagus had eaten enough, the King asked him, "Was this dish to thy mind." And when the man answered that it was indeed to his mind, certain men who had had commandment to do this thing brought the head and the hands and the feet, covered with their cover. These stood before Harpagus, and bade him uncover and take what he would. And when Harpagus so did, he saw what remained of his son. Yet, seeing it, he was not amazed, but still commanded himself. Then the King enquired of him, "Knowest thou what beast this is, of whom thou hast eaten?" And Harpagus made answer, "I know it; and all that the King doeth is well." Then he took what was left of the flesh and carried it with him to his house, and buried it.

CHAPTER VI

CYRUS OVERTHROWETH ASTYAGES AND TAKETH THE KINGDOM TO HIMSELF

WHEN King Astyages had punished Harpagus for his transgression in this fashion, he took counsel what he should do with Cyrus. Wherefore he sent for the same Magians who had interpreted to him his dream concerning his daughter. And when they were come, Astyages enquired of them how they interpreted the dream. And they spake again after the former fashion, saying that it was signified by this dream that the boy must needs be a king, if he should live to be of full age. And when they had so spoken the King spake thus to them, "The child is yet alive; and it came to pass that in the village wherein he liveth the lads his companions made him their king. And being so made, he did all things that they who are verily kings are wont to do; for he made some body-guards, and some porters, and some bearers of messages; and to others he gave other offices. Think ye that this hath aught to do with our matter?" The Magians said, "If the child is yet alive and was made king after this fashion, but not of any set

purpose of thine, thou mayest be of good courage; for
he will not be a king again. And indeed it happeneth
oftentimes that oracles and dreams and the like have
their fulfillment after this manner in little things, and so
come to nothing." To this Astyages made answer again,
"I, too, O Magians, am myself also greatly inclined to
this opinion of the matter, that the dream was fulfilled
when the boy was called by the name of a king, and
that there is no cause why I should fear him any more.
Nevertheless consider the matter well, and advise me
how I shall best order these things both for my own
house and also for you." Then the Magians said again,
"O King, it is not thy gain only but ours also that thy
kingdom should be established. For verily if it go to this
boy, it will pass away from our nation, seeing he is a
Persian; and if it so pass, then shall we be as strangers,
and shall be of no account in comparison of the Persians.
But if thou art established in thy kingdom, seeing that
thou art of the same country, then shall it in some
sort be ours; and we also shall receive great honours
at thy hands. Wherefore we should by all means take
thought for thee and for thy dominion. And now, if we
perceived beforehand any peril, surely we should not
hide it from thee; but seeing that the dream which made
thee afraid hath ended in nothing, we are ourselves of
good courage, and would bid thee also be of the same.
As for this boy, send him away out of thy sight to the
land of the Persians, even to his father and his mother."
When Astyages heard this, he rejoiced exceedingly, and
when he had called Cyrus to him he said, "My son, I
sought to do thee wrong by reason of a dream that I

had, which dream hath failed of its accomplishment; and now seeing that thy good luck hath saved thee, go thy way in peace to the Persians, and I will send some to take thee on thy way. There wilt thou find thy father and thy mother; and these not such as are the herdsman and his wife."

Then Astyages sent away Cyrus to Persia, to his father and mother, who received him with great joy, for they had thought that he was dead. And when he grew to manhood, there could not be found among his fellows that were of like age one that had such courage and virtue, and was in such favour with all men. Then, after a while, there came to him messengers with gifts from Harpagus; for the man desired exceedingly to have vengeance upon Astyages, but knew not how, being but a private man, he could gain his end; seeing therefore that Cyrus was grown to such excellence, he sought to make friendship and alliance with the young man; for he judged that they had suffered wrong, both of them, at the hands of the King. And indeed he had before this wrought for the same end. For Astyages was wont to deal cruelly with his people, and Harpagus had talked with certain of the chief men of the Medes, persuading them that they should rebel against Astyages and make Cyrus king in his stead. Now therefore, all things being ready, he sought to have communication with Cyrus and show him his purpose, but knew not how he should do it seeing that the roads were guarded. But at the last he devised this device. He took a hare, and ripped up the beast, but took not from it the skin, and having written on a roll all that he would say to Cyrus, put the roll within and sewed up again the belly of the beast. Then he equipped one of his household, that he judged to be the most faithful, as for hunting, giving him nets and the like, and with them the hare. This man, therefore, he sent into the land of Persia, and instructed him by word of mouth that he should give the hare into the hands of Cyrus, and should bid him open it himself when no man should be near. All this was done as he would have it; and Cyrus, having received the hare, opened it with his own hand, and having found the roll, read it. Now Harpagus had written in the roll these words: "Son of Cambyses, seeing that the Gods have a care for thee, for else thou hadst not come to such prosperity, bethink thee how thou mayest have vengeance on Astyages, who would have slain thee. For indeed, as regards him, thou hadst died long ago, but yet through the favour of the Gods and my help thou livest. For I judge that thou hast now for a long time known the truth about thyself, and what I have suffered at the hands of Astyages, because I slew thee not, but rather gave thee to the herdsman. Now, therefore, if thou wilt hearken to me, thou shalt be master of all the country which King Astyages now hath. Persuade the Persians that they revolt, and make war against the Medes. And it shall happen as thou wouldst have it, whether I be set by Astyages to command the army that shall be sent against thee, or whether any other of the principal men among the Medes be so set. For they will be the first to rebel against him, and will do what they can to the end that they may overthrow Astyages. All things therefore are ready. Only whatever thou doest thou shouldest do quickly."

When Cyrus had read these words he took counsel with himself how he might best cause the Persians to revolt. And having considered the matter, he did thus. He wrote in a roll what things he would; and then, having called an assembly of the Persians, opened the roll before them all, and read from it that Astyages had made him commander of the Persians. And when he had read these words he said, "Hearken now, ye Persians; come on the morrow, each man with a reaping-hook." And on the morrow when they came, each man with his reaping-hook, to a certain place in the land of Persia which was covered with thorns and briers, he said to them, "Clear ye me this place of these thorns by sunset," and the place was of eighteen or, it may be, twenty furlongs each way. So the Persians cleared the place as they had been commanded. Then Cyrus said to them, "Come again to me to-morrow, but come ready for a feast;" and he prepared a great feast for the whole army of the Persians, with flesh of goats, and sheep, and oxen, and good store of wine, and all manner of victual, the best that could be provided. And when the Persians were come on the morrow, he made them sit down in a meadow that he had, and feasted them there. And when their meal was ended, Cyrus asked them, saying, "Tell me, on which day did ye fare the better, yesterday or to-day?" And they answered, "We cannot compare the two, for yesterday we had toil and trouble, but to-day all good things." Then did Cyrus unfold to them his whole counsel, saying, "Men of Persia, the matter stands thus. If ye will hearken to me ye shall have all these good things and others also without number, and that without any need of toiling as slaves. But if ye will not hearken, ye shall have labours without end, such as ye had yesterday. Hearken therefore to me, and be free. For I am sure that I was born by the will of the Gods to bring these things to pass; and as for you, I hold that you are in no wise worse than the Medes, whether as regards valour in battle or as regards other things. I bid you, therefore, rebel this day against King Astyages."

Cyrus spake these words, and the Persians hearkened unto him right willingly, taking him for their leader, for they had long since borne it ill that they should be servants to the Medes. And when Astyages heard of these things he sent a messenger to Cyrus commanding him that he should come to him. But Cyrus said to the man, "Say to Astyages, 'Cyrus will come to thee sooner than thou wouldest have him.'" When Astyages heard these words, he gathered together all the host of the Medes, and made Harpagus captain of the host, forgetting all the wrong that he had done to him, for it was as if the Gods had smitten him with madness. Now it came to pass that when the battle was joined, some of the Medes fought with all their might against the Persians, knowing nothing of the counsels of Harpagus, and some deserted to the Persians, but the greater part turned their backs and fled. But Astyages, when he knew that the host had fled before the Persians in shameful fashion, yet lost not hope, but sent to Cyrus, threatening him and saying, "Thou shalt not go unpunished." Then he gathered together all the Medes that were left in the city, both the old men and the lads, and led them out against the Persians and fought with them. But the Medes fled a second time before the Persians, and Astyages was taken captive. And when he was brought into the camp, Harpagus stood before him, rejoicing over him and reviling him, saying, "See now, thou didst give me the flesh of my son for meat, and lo! thou hast gained for thyself slavery in the place of a kingdom." Then Astyages looked upon him and said, "Sayest thou then that this deed of Cyrus is of thy doing?" "Yea," said Harpagus, "for I devised the thing for him, and rightly claim it for my own." Then Astyages made answer, "Surely then thou art more foolish and wicked than all other men. More foolish art thou, for if thou hast done this thing of thyself and so mightest have made thyself a King, why didst thou suffer the power to go to another? And more wicked, seeing that thou hast brought all the nation of the Medes into slavery, bearing anger against me for the little matter of a feast. For if thou must needs give the kingdom to another rather than keep it for thyself, yet surely thou hadst done well to give it to a Mede rather than to a Persian. But now thou hast brought it about that the Medes, though they were innocent in this matter, having been masters aforetime are now servants, and that the Persians, having been before our servants, are now our masters." Thus was Astyages driven from his kingdom, having reigned thirty and five years, and by reason of his tyranny having brought great loss to the whole nation of the Medes. Howbeit he suffered nothing at the hands of Cyrus, but lived in peace till the day of his death.

Of the Persians, of their customs and manner of life,

there are some things worthy to be told. They have no images of the Gods, nor temples, nor altars, charging with folly them that use such things, for they hold that the Gods have not the form of men. Their custom is to go up to the tops of the highest mountains that they know, and there do sacrifice to Zeus; but by Zeus is signified the whole circle of the heavens. Also they do sacrifice to the sun, and to the moon, and to the earth, and to fire, and to water, and to the winds. And when they do sacrifice it is not lawful for any man to pray for good things for himself only, but he prays for them for the whole nation of the Persians and for the King, remembering that he is one of the Persians, and that so he prayeth for himself. They take great account of birthdays, every man making a feast, according to his means, on his own day. When they have great matters in hand they deliberate upon them, first drinking themselves drunk. But on the morrow, the master of the house where they are layeth before them, being then sober, that which they have resolved, and if it still please them, then it is confirmed. And all things on which they have deliberated being sober, they consider again when they are drunk.

Their children they teach three things only, beginning when they are five years old and continuing until twenty years; and the things are these—to ride on horseback, and to shoot with the bow, and to speak the truth.

They hold that the most shameful thing that a man can do is to lie; and next to this that he should owe money to another; for they say that the man that oweth money to another cannot choose but lie.

CHAPTER VII

THE CITY OF BABYLON, CYRUS TAKETH IT

WHEN Cyrus had overthrown the kingdom of the Lydians, and had conquered also such countries and cities as had appertained thereto, he made war in the next place against the Assyrians. Now the Assyrians have many other great and famous cities, but the greatest and most famous of all is BABYLON, for there, when Nineveh was destroyed, was set up the palace of the King. The city of Babylon is built foursquare, and the measure of each side is one hundred and twenty furlongs. Round about the walls there is a ditch, very deep and broad and full of water; and after the ditch there is a wall, of which the breadth is seventy and five feet, and the height three hundred feet. On the top of the wall, at the sides thereof, are built houses of one story, being so much apart that a chariot with four horses may turn in the space. And in the wall there are a hundred gates, of brass all of them, with posts and lintels of the same. The city is divided into two parts, between which floweth the river. Now the name of this river is Euphrates, and it cometh out of the land of Armenia, and floweth into the Red Sea.

On either side the wall is pushed forward into the river; also along each bank of the river there runneth a wall of baked brick, The city is built with houses of three stories or four, these being ordered in straight streets that cross each other. And wheresoever a street goeth down to the river there are gates of brass in the wall of brick that is by the riverside, gates for each street. Also over and above the outer wall of the city there is an inner wall, of wellnigh equal strength, but in thickness not so great.

In each part of the city there was a great building, of which one was the King's palace and the other the temple of Belus. This temple hath brazen gates, and is foursquare, being two furlongs every way. In the midst there is a tower which is solid throughout and of the bigness of a furlong each way; and on this tower is built another tower, and yet another upon this, and so forth, seven in all. Round about these towers are built stairs; and for one who hath climbed halfway a landing-place and chairs where he may rest; and in the topmost tower there is a temple very splendidly furnished, and a couch and a table thereby, but no image.

There is another temple below, and in it a statue of Zeus sitting, and before it a table of gold; the throne and the steps are also of gold; and the weight of all is eight hundred talents. Outside is a golden altar, on which a thousand talents of frankincense were wont to be burnt at the great feast. Here also was a great statue of gold, twelve cubits high, and solid throughout. This statue Darius was minded to take, but dared not; yet did Xerxes take it, and slew the priest that would have hindered him.

Of this city of Babylon there have been many kings, and two queens. Of these queens the first made for the river great banks, for before her day it used to overflow all the plain of Babylon. The name of this Queen was Semiramis, and the name of the second Queen was Nitetis. This Nitetis, seeing that the kingdom of the Medes increased daily, and that they were not content with what they had, but sought to subdue others, and had conquered many cities, among which was Nineveh, devised a defence against them. For first she caused that the river Euphrates, which before had flowed in a straight course, should now fetch a compass; and this she did by making for it new channels. And now one that saileth on this river cometh thrice in three days to the self-same village, and the name of this village is Ardericca. Also she made a great lake, digging it out by the side of the river; and the circuit of this lake is four hundred and twenty furlongs. Now both these things she did for the same end, that the stream of the river might be the slower and the voyage to Babylon a voyage of many windings, and that when the voyage on the river should be ended, then there should be the voyage on the lake. All this was done on that side of the city which looketh towards the country of the Medes; for she would not that the Medes should come into her dominion and learn her affairs. Also she did this great work for the city. There being two parts, and the river flowing between them, the citizens had been wont in days of former kings to cross, if they had need, from the one part to the other in boats; and this was a toil to them. She caused her servants to cut very large stones, and when these were finished, she commanded that they should turn the river into the lake which she had dug. And while this was a-filling, the old stream being now dry, she embanked with brick the side of the river, and the ways also that led thereto from the gates. But in the middle part of the city she built a bridge with the stones which she had caused to be cut, binding them together with iron and lead. On this bridge there were laid, so long as it was day, four-cornered timbers, on the which the men of Babylon crossed the bridge. But at nightfall the timbers were taken away, so that the people of the city might not steal from each other. And when this was finished she brought the river again into his channel.

This queen devised this deceit. She made for herself a tomb over that one of the gates by which the people were chiefly wont to go forth. On this tomb she wrote certain words of which the significance was this: "IF ONE OF THE KINGS AFTER ME LACK MONEY, LET HIM OPEN THIS TOMB AND TAKE WHAT HE WILL. BUT LET HIM NOT OPEN IT UNLESS HE NEED, FOR IT WILL BE THE WORSE FOR HIM." This tomb no man would meddle with till Darius came to the kingdom. Now it seemed a grievous thing to Darius that no man should use the gate, and that money should be there, and that it should call men to take it, yet should not be taken. For no one used the gate because there was a dead body above his head as he went out. Wherefore he opened the tomb; but having opened it, found no money therein, but only the dead body of the queen and these words, saying, "IF THOU WERE NOT INSATIATE OF MONEY AND A LOVER OF GAIN, THOU HADST NOT OPENED THE RESTING-PLACE OF THE DEAD."

Now the king against whom Cyrus made war was the son of this woman, and his name was Labynetus; and this had been the name of his father also. Now when the Great King, the King of the Persians, marcheth anywhither he is well provided with food and cattle, and also with water from the river Choaspes, which floweth by the city of Susa; for the King drinketh not of any other river save this only. And many four-wheeled waggons, drawn by mules, follow the army whithersoever it goeth, bearing vessels of silver wherein is the water, having been first boiled. But when Cyrus came in his march to the river Gyndes (this river floweth into the Tigris) there befell this thing. While he was seeking to cross the river, which is of such bigness that ships can sail thereon, one of the white horses which are sacred would have crossed the river by swimming, and in so doing was drowned. Then Cyrus was very wroth with the river that had done him this wrong; and sware that he would make it so weak that a woman should be able to cross it without wetting her knee. When he had sworn this oath he divided his army into two parts, and commanded each part that it should dig long trenches by the side of the river—one part working on each side—and the number of the trenches should be one hundred and eighty for each part. And as there was a

great multitude of men the work was accomplished in
no great space of time; nevertheless they consumed the
whole summer in this work. So the river Gyndes was
made to flow into these trenches, three hundred and
sixty in all. And when this was done, and the winter
was over, together with the next spring Cyrus led his
army to Babylon. And when he came near to the city,
the Babylonians came forth to meet him; and when the
battle was joined, the Babylonians fled before Cyrus,
and were shut up in their city. Now they had gathered
provisions for many years, for they knew that Cyrus
was a man of war, and sought to conquer all the nations
round about. So, therefore, their walls also being very
strong, they took no account of the siege; but Cyrus was
much troubled, for even after a long time he had done
nothing in the matter of taking the city. And whether
he himself devised the device, or another devised it
for him, cannot be said; but this he did. He divided his
army into two portions; and of these he set one above
the city where the river floweth into it, and the other
he set below it where the river floweth out. To these he
gave commandment that when they should see the river
so shallow that a man could cross it they should enter
the city by it. And when he had thus ordered things, he
himself departed with such of the army as were of no
account for war, and when he came to the lake which
Nitetis, Queen of Babylon, had made by the riverside,
then did he thus. He made a great trench, and turned
the river into the lake, which in those days was a marsh
only and not filled with water. And when this had been
done the river became shallow, so that a man might

cross it, and the Persians to whom the commandment had been given, perceiving what had happened, and that the water now came but up to the middle of a man's thigh, entered the city of Babylon by way of the river. Now if the men of Babylon had known beforehand or perceived the thing that Cyrus was doing, then all these Persians had perished miserably, for they would have shut all the gates leading down to the river, and would have gone up themselves on to the walls that were built along the banks of the river, and so would have had the Persians as it were in a fish-trap. But in truth the Persians came upon them unawares. Now the bigness of the city was such that they who dwelt in the middle parts knew not that the outside parts had been taken; but played and danced and delighted themselves, till indeed they were made to know it in such fashion as they liked not.

This land of Babylon is a very good land. For while all the rest of Asia nourisheth the Great King and his army for eight months, this alone nourisheth him for four months. And there cometh to him that holdeth this province under the King, a measure of silver containing twelve gallons day by day. Rain falleth not often, but the plain is watered by the river, as is also the land of Egypt; and it beareth wheat as doth no other country in the whole earth, even two hundredfold, and when the harvest is of the best, three hundredfold.

They have this law about marriage. In every village and town they gather together such maidens as are of a marriageable age into one place, the multitude of men standing in a circle round about them. Then there

BABYLONIAN CAPTIVES

standeth up a herald in the midst and selleth them, one by one; and the manner of selling them is this. First he taketh her that is counted the fairest in the whole company, and when she has been sold for a great sum of money, then her that is the next in fairness. Then all the wealthy men among the Babylonians, being minded to marry, contend with each other who shall buy those that excel in beauty; but such of the common folk as are minded to marry care not at all for beauty, but take the maidens that are less comely to look upon, and money with them. For when the herald hath finished his selling of the beautiful maidens, then he taketh her that is worst favoured in the company, or, it may be, maimed of a limb, and offereth her. And the men say for how much money they will take her to wife; and to him that saith the least is she given. And the gold that the rich men pay for the well-favoured among the maidens, this do the poor men receive with the ill-favoured. Nor is

73

it lawful for a man to give his daughter in marriage to any that he will.

Another excellent custom have they with them that are sick. These they carry forth from their houses into the market-place; for they have no physicians in their country. Then all that come near give their counsel about the sick man, if any one hath himself endured such disease as the sick man hath, or hath seen any other enduring it. And they tell each of them in their turn how they were cured of such disease, or may have seen others cured. But it is not lawful for any to pass by the sick man till he shall have made enquiry what his disease may be.

CHAPTER VIII

CYRUS MAKETH WAR AGAINST THE MASSAGETÆ, AND DIETH

WHEN Cyrus had conquered the Babylonians and taken their city, it came into his heart to make war against the Massagetæ and to subdue them. This is a very great and valiant nation, dwelling towards the sunrising, beyond the river Araxes. This Araxes is a great river, having in it islands that are of the bigness of Lesbos. In these islands, which are, they say, many in number, there dwell men who eat in the summer all manner of roots, but for the winter they store up such fruits as they have found to be good for food. They have among them one tree that beareth fruits of a very wonderful kind. The men assemble in companies and light a fire, and sit round the fire in a circle; then they throw upon this fire of the fruit of the tree; and when they smell the savour of the fruit that is thrown upon the fire, they grow drunken with the smell thereof, even, as the Greeks grow drunken with wine; and more fruit being thrown upon the fire they grow yet more drunken, till at the last they come to dancing and singing. In the marshes of this river where it floweth into the sea—and it floweth, they say, through forty mouths—there dwell men that have fish only for food, eating them raw, and for clothing they have the skins of seals.

Now the cause wherefore Cyrus had it in his mind to make war against the Massagetæ was this: that his spirit was puffed up and exalted with many things, as with his birth, from which he judged that he was above the measure of a man, and with his good luck that had followed him in his wars; for of all the nations against whom he had been minded to make war not one had been able to escape. Now the ruler of the Massagetæ in those days was a woman, whose husband was dead, and the name of this woman was Tomyris. Cyrus therefore sent messengers to her, saying that he would fain take her to wife. But Tomyris, knowing that he wished not for her but for the kingdom of the Massagetæ, denied herself to him. Then Cyrus, when he could not prevail by craft, marched to the river Araxes, and made war openly against the Massagetæ, for he began to make bridges of ships over the river by which his army might be able to cross, and to build also towers for defence upon the ships. But while he was busying himself with these things, Queen Tomyris sent to him, saying, "O King of the Medes, cease from doing these things that thou art doing; for thou canst not know whether they will be to thy profit. Cease from them therefore, and rule thy own people, and be content also to see me ruling over my people. Yet, as I know that thou wilt not follow this my counsel, and that there is nothing that is less to thy mind than to be at peace, I offer thee this. If thou greatly desirest to make trial of the strength of the Massagetæ, then cease from this thy labour of making bridges across the Araxes, and when we have gone back three days' march from the river, then take thy army across; or, if thou wouldst rather have it so, do thou on thy part go back three days' journey from the river, and abide our coming."

When Cyrus heard this, he called together the chief men of the Persians, and laid the whole matter before them, enquiring of them which of these two things he should rather do. For the most part the counsel of the Persians agreed together that he should suffer Tomyris and her army to enter his country. But Crœsus the Lydian, being present in the council, agreed not with this opinion, but gave contrary advice, saying, "I have said to thee aforetime, O King, that from the day when Zeus made thee lord over me, I cease not to turn away, if it may be, any evil that I may perceive coming upon thy house. And, indeed, my own troubles have been hard teachers to me. Now, therefore, if thou countest thyself to be immortal and the army which thou rulest to be immortal also, there shall be no need that I should show forth my opinion. But if thou knowest thyself to be a man only, and thine army to be of men only, then consider that there is as it were a wheel of the fortunes of men, and that this wheel turneth round always, and suffereth not the same man to be always in prosperity. Now, my opinion is contrary to the opinion of these. If thou sufferest these men to come into thy country, there is this peril. If thou fleest before them, then thou losest thy whole kingdom. But if, on the contrary, thou comest into their country and they flee before thee, then thou wilt conquer them altogether. Also, it doth not become thee, being such an one as Cyrus the son of Cambyses, to give place before a woman. But hearken now unto me, and I will tell thee what thou shalt do. These Massagetæ have no knowledge of the good things of the Persians. Do thou, therefore, kill for these men great store of sheep, and cause their flesh to be cooked, and furnish a feast for them in our camp. Forget not also to fill bowls with wine without stint, and to set out all manner of good things. Which when thou hast done, leave there in the camp that which is of least account in thy army, and go back again with that which remains to the river. For I am persuaded that these men, when they see these good things, will fly forthwith upon them, and that we shall find occasion to do great things against them."

Then Cyrus rejected the former counsel, and chose the counsel of Crœsus. Wherefore he sent a message to Queen Tomyris, that she should depart from the river, for that he was resolved to cross over into her country. After this he called his son Cambyses, to whom also he had left the kingdom after him, and committed Crœsus into his hands, bidding him deal kindly with him and honour him, if he should not prosper in battle with the Massagetæ. And when he had sent these two away into the land of Persia, he himself crossed the river Araxes with his army.

In the night after he had crossed the river he saw a vision in his sleep, and the vision was this. He saw the eldest of the sons of Hystaspes, having wings upon his shoulders, with one whereof he shadowed the whole land of Asia, and with the other the whole land of Europe. Now, the eldest of the sons of Hystaspes, who was of the house of Achæmenes, was Darius, being then about twenty years of age; and he had been left in the land of Persia as not being of age to go with the host. And Cyrus, when he woke from sleep, considered with himself what this vision might mean; and because it seemed to him a very great matter, he called Hystaspes, and taking him apart by himself, said to him, "Hystaspes, thy son is manifestly proved to be laying plots against me and my kingdom. And how I know this thing thou shalt hear. The Gods have great care for me, and show me beforehand all things that shall come to pass. Now, therefore, in this night past I saw a vision in my sleep—even the eldest of thy sons with wings upon his shoulders, with one whereof he shadowed the land of Asia, and with the other the land of Europe. Seeing then that I have had this vision, it must needs be that he is laying plots against me. Do thou, therefore, depart with all speed into the land of Persia, and see that when I shall have subdued this country and am returned, he shall be brought to the trial." This said Cyrus thinking that Darius was laying plots against him. But in very truth the Gods showed him by this vision that he should die in that land, and that his kingdom should be given to Darius. Then Hystaspes made answer, "My lord the King, the Gods forbid that there should be any Persian who would plot against thee, and if such there be, may he be brought to nought. For thou hast made the Persians free who were slaves before, and to be the rulers of all men in place of being ruled by others. If, therefore, it be signified by this vision that my son is plotting against thee, be sure that I will deliver him to thee to do with him as thou wilt." When Hystaspes had said this, he crossed the Araxes and went his way into the land of Persia, that he might keep Darius his son against King Cyrus should return. And when Cyrus had gone a day's march from the river Araxes, he did according to the word of Crœsus, For he returned with the better part of his army to the river and left the worse part behind. Then there came a third part of the army of the Massagetæ, and fought with those that Cyrus had left behind, and slew them. And when they had vanquished their enemies, seeing the feast that had been prepared, they sat down and feasted; and having filled themselves with food and wine, they lay down to sleep. But while they slept the Persians came upon them, and slew many of them, and took yet more of them alive. And among them that they took was the captain of the host of the Massagetæ, being a son of Queen Tomyris, whose name was Spargapises. And when the queen knew what had befallen the army and her son also, she sent unto Cyrus, saying, "Be not puffed up, O Cyrus, thou that never canst be satisfied with blood, by reason of this thing that thou hast done. For thou hast taken of the fruit of the vine, with which ye are wont to fill yourselves to madness, so that when the wine enters into you, there come forth from you all manner of evil words; this, I say, thou hast taken, and with it hast prevailed over my son, vanquishing him by craft, and not by strength. Now, therefore, I give thee this counsel. Give back to me my son, and go thy way out of this land unhurt, having worked thy will upon the third part of the army of the Massagetæ. But if thou wilt not do according to my words, then I swear by the Sun, who is the lord of the Massagetæ, that though thou canst not be satisfied with blood, yet will I satisfy thee." But Cyrus, when this message was brought to him, took no heed of it. After this, Spargapises, the son of Queen Tomyris, when the wine had left him, and he knew into what trouble he had come, made entreaty to Cyrus that he might be loosed awhile from his bonds. But so soon as ever he was loosed, he slew himself.

After this Queen Tomyris, seeing that Cyrus would not listen to her counsel, gathered together all her army, and joined battle with the Persians. And of all battles that have ever been fought among barbarians was never one fiercer than this battle. First they stood apart and shot at each other with bows; and when their arrows were spent, they fell upon each other with spears and swords, and so fought. For a long time they contended against each other, and neither the one nor the other would give place. But at the last the Massagetæ prevailed over the Persians. And the greater part of the army of the Persians perished on that day, and Cyrus himself also was slain, having reigned, twenty and eight years. Then Queen Tomyris, having first filled a skin with man's blood, commanded that they should search among the dead bodies for the body of Cyrus. And when they had found it, she cut off his head and thrust it into the skin, and scoffed at the dead body, saying, "Thou didst take my son by craft when I could have prevailed over thee in battle; and now, as I sware, I will satisfy thee with blood."

Thus Cyrus the son of Cambyses the Persian died in the land of the Massagetæ, and Cambyses his son reigned in his stead.

CHAPTER IX

OF THE MANNERS OF THE EGYPTIANS

THERE is no country in the whole world that hath in it more marvellous things or greater works of buildings and the like than hath the land of Egypt. And as the heavens in this land are such as other men know not— for in the upper parts there falls not rain but once in a thousand years or more, and in the lower parts not often—and the river is different from all other rivers in the earth, seeing that it overflows in the summer and is at its least in the winter, so also do the manners of the Egyptians differ from the manners of all other men. For among them the women buy and sell in the market, but the men sit at home and spin. And even in this matter of spinning they do not as others, for others push the shuttle in the loom from below upwards, but these men push it from above downwards. Also the men carry burdens on their heads, but the women carry them on their shoulders. And the women pray to none, either god or goddess, but the men pray to all. And there is no duty laid on a son to succour father or mother, if it be not his pleasure to do it, but on a daughter there is laid, whether she will or no. In the matter of mourning for the dead these folk have a strange custom, for they let grow the hair upon the head and chin when they mourn, but are shaven at other times. And whereas other men hold themselves better than the beasts, the Egyptians have these in great honour, keeping them in their houses, aye, and worshipping them. Nor do they eat the food of other men, holding it a shame to be fed on wheat and barley which others use, and eating the grain of millet only; and the dough that it is made of, this they knead, trampling it with their feet, but mud and such like things they are wont to take up with their hands. About garments, their custom is that a man hath two but a woman only one; and in their ships and boats they fasten the sheets and ropes to the sails from within, whereas other men fasten them from without; also in their books they write not as others, from left to right, but from right to left.

INSPECTION OF CATTLE

Now as to the beasts and the honour in which the Egyptians hold them, there are many strange things to be said. The cow they reckon to be sacred to Isis the goddess, who is the same that the Greeks call so, fabling her to be a maiden whom Heré changed into the shape of a heifer. Nor will any Egyptian man or woman kiss a Greek upon the mouth, knowing that they are wont to eat cow's flesh; neither will they use any knife or spit or cauldron of a Greek, nor will they eat even of the flesh that is lawful to be eaten (for they eat of oxen, as I shall presently tell) if it be cut with the knife of a Greek. The oxen they hold to be sacred to Apis, whom the Greeks call Epaphus, saying that he was the son of Isis. These they sacrifice, if so be that they find them to be clean. And the manner of finding whether they be clean or no is this. One of the priests that is set to perform this office diligently examines the beast, both when he stands up and when he lies down, to see whether there be any black hairs on him, and if there be so much as one, then he is not clean. Then he looks at the tongue to see if it be without certain signs, and at the tail, whether the hairs be set in due order. And if he find it to be altogether clean he twisteth a reed about the horns of the beast, and putteth a seal of clay upon his forehead. And when they sacrifice it, they cut off the head, praying at the same time that if any evil thing be about to happen either to them that do the sacrifice or to the land of Egypt, it may fall rather upon this head. And of the body, some parts they burn with fire and some they eat.

Sometimes it comes to pass that there is born a bull calf that hath such a colour and such marks upon him that this people deem it to be the god Apis himself. It is black with a foursquare mark of white upon its forehead, and on its back the similitude of an eagle, and the hair on its tail double, and under its tongue a mark like unto a beetle. When such a one is born the people put on their best apparel and make great rejoicing, saying that the god hath come down to dwell among them. This thing came to pass when King Cambyses of Persia was in Egypt. Now it chanced that in those days the King was much troubled, because the army which he had sent against the men of Hammon who dwelt in the desert had wholly perished, a mighty wind from the south blowing mountains of sand upon it. And he was in great wrath to see the Egyptians making merry, for he thought that they did it in scorn of him and his troubles. And first he sent for the chief men of Memphis, for that was the city in which he chanced to be dwelling, and enquired of them why the people rejoiced; and when they said that the god had appeared among them after many years, and that the people rejoiced therefore according to custom, he answered in great anger that they had lied to him, and ordered them to be put to death as having said a thing manifestly false. Afterwards he sent for the priests, and when they answered him after the same manner, he said that he would not that a god should come to the land that could be handled and he not see him, and bade them bring him. So the priests brought the calf Apis, and the King, when he saw him, drew a dagger that he had and smote the beast on the thigh, saying to the priests, "Ye knaves! be these your gods, creatures that have flesh and blood, and can be hurt with steel? Truly such a god is worthy of the Egyptians. But surely ye shall not go unpunished."

And he bade the executioners scourge them to death, and to slay any Egyptian that they should find making merry. So the feast of the Egyptians had an end, and the calf that had been wounded lay for a while grievously sick in the temple, and so died. But when it was dead the priests buried it, taking good care that the matter should not come to the ears of the King.

Commonly when an ox dieth they bury it in the suburbs of the city with one of his horns, or it may be both, above the ground that they may know the place. And after a certain time when they judge the flesh to have altogether rotted, they take up the bones and put them into a ship, which cometh for that purpose from a certain island in the lower part of the river, where there is a temple of the goddess Aphrodite. In this place are gathered together the bones of all the oxen that die, and here are they buried. In like manner do they bring other beasts that die, for none of them do they kill, save only in sacrifice.

As to sacrifice, indeed, they follow different customs in different places. Thus they that are of the region of Thebes sacrifice goats, but will have nothing to do with sheep; and, on the other hand, they that are of the region of Mende sacrifice sheep, but hold goats to be unclean.

The crocodile some of the Egyptians hold to be sacred, but not all. And in every city where they hold it, as in Thebes and in the cities round about the lake Moeris, they keep one crocodile to which they do special honour. This they train to be tame to the hand,

and they put earrings of glass and of gold into his ears, and bracelets on his fore feet, and give it a portion of food day by day, and make offerings to it, and when it dies they embalm it and bury it in the sacred sepulchres. But the people that dwell in the city of Elephantiné count them not to be sacred at all, but slay them and eat them.

Of hunting them there are many ways, but the most noteworthy is this. The hunter fastens a chine of swine's flesh upon a hook, and casts it into the middle of the river. After this he takes a live pig and beats it by the banks of the river. And the crocodile, hearing the crying of the pig, makes for the place, and chancing on the hook with the swine's flesh swallows it down. Then the men drag it to land. But so soon as ever it touches the land the hunter daubeth the eye of the beast with mud. If he do this, then will he easily do what he will with it; but if not, he hath much trouble.

The river-horse, which is a great beast, as big as the biggest of oxen, having an ox's hoof, only cloven, and the mane and tail and voice of a horse, the people of one region hold to be sacred, but to the rest it is common. There are water snakes in the river; these they all hold sacred, and among fish one that has great scales, and also the eel.

Among birds are sacred the fox goose (which they so call because it has a hole in the earth, such as the foxes have), and the ibis, which the Egyptians honour because it fights against the winged serpents. For they say that in the spring-time a great multitude of winged serpents cometh out of the land of Arabia seeking to pass into Egypt, and that the ibis meet them in a narrow way which there is between Arabia and Egypt, and will not let them pass. But the most sacred of all birds is the phœnix. This bird men do not often see, for it cometh, they say, into the land of Egypt but once in five hundred years. And the manner of his coming is this, according to the report of the country, though, indeed, it is a thing hard to be believed. He bringeth his father, covered round about with myrrh, to the temple of the Sun, and burieth him in the temple of the Sun. And that he may do this, he first maketh a great ball of myrrh, as big as he can carry, making trial of what he can do in carrying. And when he hath finished the trial and can carry such weight as is needed, he holloweth out the ball, and putteth his father within, and addeth thereto such myrrh as he has taken from within. And the weight, they say, is the same as it was before. The feathers of this bird are in part golden and in part red: and it hath the shape and bigness of an eagle.

Of the beasts that are held sacred there are keepers appointed, both men and women; and this office the son inheriteth from his father and the daughter from her mother. When a man maketh a vow to the god to whom a beast is counted to belong, and the time is come that he should pay it, he shaves the heads of his children, or the half, or, it may be, the third part of their heads, according to the letter of his vow. Then he weigheth the hair that hath been cut of against silver, and payeth the silver to the keeper of the beast, who buyeth food for it, fish or the like. Thus are the beasts nourished. If a man kill a beast that is sacred, he must suffer for it. If he kill it of set purpose, then he is put to death, but if he kill it unknowingly, then he payeth a fine, such as the priests may choose to lay upon him. But if a man kill an ibis or a hawk, whether he do it of set purpose or no, he must die.

The cat the Egyptians hold in great honour. Of this beast there is a very marvellous thing to be told. When it chanceth that a house is burning a strange madness cometh upon the cats, for they are very desirous to leap into the fire. And the Egyptians set guards round about the place, if by any means they may keep the cats from their purpose; nor do they care to quench the fire, if so be that they may do this: but the cats, nevertheless, making their way through them, or leaping over them, have their will, and so perish. Over this the Egyptians make great lamentation. If a cat die in the course of nature, all that are in that house shave their eyebrows only, but all the dwellers in a house wherein a dog shall die shave their heads and whole bodies. The cats, when they are dead, they carry away for burial to the city of Bubastis, but the dogs they bury each in the city where he dies, only in the holy sepulchres. Other beasts and birds they bury elsewhere, according to the nature of each. Bears, of which there are few only, and wolves (and the wolves in this country are but little bigger than foxes) they bury where they may chance to find them.

Swine the Egyptians hold to be altogether abominable. If a man so much as touch one of these beasts in passing, he goeth straightway to the river, and dippeth himself therein and his garments also. No swineherd is permitted to enter the temple of any god, nor will any man give his daughter in marriage to a swine-herd, or take a swineherd's daughter to wife; but they marry and are given in marriage among themselves only. Notwithstanding, on a certain day, to wit, the day of

PURSUING BIRDS

the full moon, and to certain gods, that is, to the Moon and to Bacchus, they offer swine in sacrifice. And when they offer them to the Moon, after they have burnt certain parts with fire, that which remains of the flesh they eat. But on no other day would they so much as taste it. And the poor, such as for lack of means cannot buy the beast itself, make swine of dough. These they cook and offer in sacrifice, and so eat. But the swine which they offer in sacrifice to Bacchus they eat not, but give them to the swineherds from whom they may have bought them.

For food the Egyptians have bread made of millet, as has been said before. They have wine made of barley, for the vine groweth not in their land. Of birds they eat doves and pigeons, and such small kinds as there are in the country. Of fish they have a great store, not a few in the river, but yet more in lakes and ponds, where they nourish them. Of such fish as pass from the lakes into the sea there is told this thing, that such as be caught passing from the lake into the sea are found to have their heads rubbed upon the left side, and such as are caught passing from the sea to the lake have their heads rubbed upon the right. And the cause is this: that when they swim downwards they keep themselves very close to the left shore, and when they swim upwards they keep themselves very close to the right shore, not ceasing to touch it, lest haply through the flow of the stream they should miss the way, and so be lost. There is also another strange thing of the fish in Egypt. So soon as the Nile begins to rise, the hollows of the earth and the pools that are by the side of the river begin to fill, for the water runs through to them from the river. And so soon as they are full they are seen to abound with multitudes of small fishes. Whereof the cause seemeth to be this: in the year before the fish that have been in these pools and hollows run out with the water as the river falls, but leave their eggs in the mud. And these, when the season of the flood comes round again, speedily become fishes.

Such of the Egyptians as dwell in the marshes of

the river have also for food the seed of the water-lilies, which grow abundantly when the river overfloweth the plains. This seed is like to the seed of a poppy, and they make of it loaves which they bake with fire, having first dried it in the sun. Also the root of this water-lily (which they call the lotus) may be eaten, being round, and of the bigness of an apple. Other lilies there are growing in the river, like to roses, which have a fruit very like to a wasp's comb, and in it many seeds of the bigness of an olive, which the men eat both green and dry. Also these marsh folk gather the reeds, and use the upper part for other things, as for the making of paper and the like, but the lower part, as much as a cubit's length from the ground, they eat. Those who will have this dish at its best cook it in an oven red hot, and so eat it. For oil olive these people use that which they press out of the castorberry, of which they plant great store by the riverside. It serveth for lamps as oil-olive, but hath an evil smell.

It must be told how they escape from the biting of the gnats, of which there are great multitudes. For they that dwell in the upper country find help in their towers, into which they climb of a night, and so sleep in peace. But the marsh folk do not so, but every man has his cast-net, and with this he catches fish by day and hangs it over his bed by night. And if he sleep wrapped in his cloak or in a hair garment, the gnats bite through it, but through the net they bite not.

The rich men among the Egyptians have this custom at their feasts. When the meal is ended there is carried round to every one of the guests an image made of wood, shapen and painted to the likeness of a man. This image is of a cubit, or may be, two cubits in length, and is laid in a coffin. And he that beareth it saith to each man, "Look thou at this, and drink, and rejoice thy heart, for when thou diest thou shalt be such as this image."

The dead they embalm; and the manner of this embalming differeth according as the man or woman that is dead is rich or poor or between the two. But if a man be torn by a crocodile or die by drowning in the river, then, whether he be an Egyptian born or a stranger in the land, must he be embalmed with all the costliest spices that may be, and buried in the sacred sepulchres. Neither may any man touch him, whether kinsman or friend, but the priests of the Nile only. These handle him with all reverence as being more than a mortal man, and so bury him.

The Egyptians have among them a great multitude of physicians. But each man is a physician of one part of the body only; for one healeth diseases of the eyes, and another diseases of the head, and a third diseases of the teeth.

Priests are held in great honour among them. For indeed there is no nation in the whole world that is more careful to pay due reverence to the Gods and to all holy things. These priests shave their bodies every third day. They wear garments of linen and sandals of reed from the river, and other garments or sandals it is not lawful for them to have. They bathe themselves in water twice every day, and twice every night; and other things of the like kind without end do they observe. Nevertheless, they are by no means in evil case. There is no need for them to spend aught of their own possessions, for there is brought to them day by day for their food great store of the flesh of oxen and of geese. For the Egyptians keep with them great flocks of these birds, holding them to be sacred. Also they have a provision of wine, and this is not of barley, such as men commonly drink in this country, but wine of grapes. But it is not lawful for them to eat of any kind of fish, and as for beans, they may not so much as look at them; and indeed none of the Egyptians will eat of the bean.

A FLOCK OF GEESE

To each god there are many priests, and of these one is called the high priest. When a priest dieth, his son taketh his office.

All the Egyptians worship not the same gods, but Isis and Osiris they all worship; and this Osiris is the same as he whom the Greeks call Bacchus or Dionysus; and his feast is in all things like to that which the Greeks keep to their gods, only that there is no acting of plays.

As for Isis the Greeks call her Demeter, that is to say, being interpreted, Mother Earth.

Hercules the most of them worship, but not all. But this Hercules is not the same as he of whom the Greeks talk as being a hero and the son of Amphitryon of Argos, but an ancient god, and one of the twelve. For the Egyptians say that there were in the beginning eight gods, and that of these eight were born other twelve; and that it is seventeen thousand years reckoned to the days of King Amasis, of whom mention will be made hereafter, since these twelve were born. Also in Tyre of Phœnicia there is a temple of Hercules, very noble, in which are many gifts and offerings, and especially two pillars, the one of pure gold and the other of emerald, which shines mightily by night. The priests of this temple affirm that it was built at the very beginning, together with the city itself; and that as for the city, there were two thousand years and more from its building to the days of King Amasis. Neither doth this agree with what the Greeks say of Hercules; and as for what they tell of his doings in Egypt, it is a vain thing and altogether incredible. For they say that coming to Egypt he was taken of a great multitude of the people, and crowned with garlands, and led to the altar of Zeus, to the intent that he might be sacrificed; and that he submitted himself to them till he came to the altar itself, but that being there, he turned upon them and slew them all. Now, it is not lawful for the Egyptians to sacrifice any animal save only sheep and oxen and calves and geese. How, then, could they sacrifice a man? And how could Hercules, being but one, and a mortal

OSIRIS

man—for the Greeks count him to have been—slay thousands?

Ares they worship in other cities and in Papremis, in which last place they follow this custom. The image of the god, which abides in a small shrine of wood covered over with gold, they carry out on the day before the feast from the temple to another of the holy places. And on the day of the feast, when the sun is now drawing near to his setting, they put the image and its shrine on a waggon with four wheels, and drag him towards the temple. Now in the front of the temple there is ranged a multitude of men, having all of them clubs of wood in their hands. These seek to hinder the priests that drag the waggon and the image from entering the temple. And there is ranged upon the other side of the court another multitude, of a thousand men and more, having also clubs of wood in their hands. These busy themselves with the saying of prayers. But when they see that the god is hindered from entering his temple, they come to his help and the help of his priests. Upon this there ariseth a very fierce battle, the men striking each other with their clubs of wood, and breaking each others' heads. And it is to be believed that many die of their wounds, yet the Egyptians affirm that no man so dieth.

Let so much then be said about the Egyptians and their customs and manner of life, and the gods whom they worship.

CHAPTER X

OF CERTAIN KINGS OF EGYPT

OF all the kings of Egypt there has been none greater than Sesostris. This man made ships of war, and sailing down the Red Sea conquered the nations that dwelt upon its shores. And this he did till he could sail no further by reason of the shallows. And in the land of each nation that he conquered he set up a pillar with an inscription with his own name, speaking honourably of such as had fought bravely against him, and with scorn of such as had not quitted themselves like men. And thus he passed through the whole land of Asia, and from Asia he crossed over into Europe. And when he had subdued this also as far as Scythia and Thrace, he turned back to Egypt, and coming to the river Phasis, which floweth into the Black Sea by the way of the east, he left there a certain part of his army; but whether he did this to take possession of that country, or that the men were wearied with their wanderings, cannot be known. Coming back to Egypt, he brought with him a great multitude of men of all the nations whom he had conquered. And when he came to Daphnæ, his brother, whom he had made king in his stead, called him and his wife and children to a banquet. But while Sesostris sat at meat, the brother piled wood about the banqueting-house and set fire to it. Then Sesostris took counsel with his wife how they might be saved. And she said that he should slay two out of the number of his sons, for he had six in all, and using them as a bridge should so pass over the fire. This he did and escaped, he and his wife and four of his sons. After this, having first punished his brother, he appointed work to the multitude of men whom he had brought with him, to drag great blocks of stone for the building of temples, and to dig canals. For before the days of Sesostris horses and chariots could pass over the land of Egypt; but after him they could not, though indeed it is a plain country, so divided is it by canals. This the King did that he might bring the water of the river to such towns as lie far from it. Sesostris also divided the land of Egypt in equal plots among the inhabitants. These paid dues for their land year by year, and so the King had his revenue. And if the river carried away any part of a man's plot, he told the matter to the King. Then the King would send men to measure the plot; and according as it was found to be less, the less was demanded of the man. And thus was the art of geometry, that is to say, the measuring of land, first known in Egypt.

Many years after Sesostris there reigned King Proteus. In his days, as the Egyptians say, came Paris to Egypt, bringing with him Queen Helen, whom he had carried off from Menelaüs her husband. For the Egyptian story of Paris is this, being wholly different from that which Homer hath in his Iliad. When Paris had sailed from Sparta, and was now in the midst of the Ægean Sea, a storm arose, and carried him to the land of Egypt. Being arrived here he disembarked at a place which was called the "Saltpans," near to the mouth of the Nile that is called Canopus. Here there stood on the shore, and, indeed, stands to this day, a temple of Hercules. And the custom of the temple is, that if a slave runs away from his master, and has certain marks made upon him, he belongeth to the god, and his master may not lay hand upon him. So the slaves of Paris left him and fled to the temple, and that they might do him damage with the King, they told the whole story of Queen Helen to the priest of the temple, and to the captain of the river, a certain Thonis. This Thonis sent to the King, saying, "There hath come to this land a certain stranger of Troy, who hath done a wicked deed in the land of Greece, for from one who showed him hospitality he hath taken away his wife, and great riches also with her. Wilt thou then that we let him depart unharmed, or that we take from him that which he hath?" King Proteus made answer, "I will that ye bring this man who hath so wronged his host before me, that I may hear what he shall say." So Thonis took Paris and Helen, and the riches that they had with them, and the slaves also. Then the King asked Paris who he was and whence he had come. And Paris answered that he was a man of Troy, and that he sailed from Sparta. But when the King would know whence he had taken Queen Helen, he was confused, speaking things that were not true. But when the King had heard from the slaves the whole story, he gave sentence in this manner: "I am steadfastly purposed not to put to death any stranger who may be carried out of his course by stormy winds to this country; otherwise I had surely avenged this fault on thee. For indeed thou art the wickedest of men, that hast so wronged thy host, stealing from him his wife, and also robbing him of much treasure. Thee indeed I slay not, for I would not slay any stranger, but I suffer thee not to have this woman or this treasure. These will I keep for the host himself, till he shall himself come and take them, if he will. But as to thee and thy comrades, I bid you depart from my land within three days, and if not, ye shall be dealt with as enemies."

Now that Homer had heard this tale of the coming of Paris into Egypt may be taken for certain, being manifest from this that in the book of "The Valiant Deeds of Diomed" he speaketh thus: "There were robes of many colours, the work of women of Sidon, which the noble Paris brought thence in the voyage whereon he carried with him Queen Helen, sailing over the broad sea." Also in the "Wanderings of Ulysses," he saith: "Such marvelous medicine had the daughter of Zeus; good medicine which Polydamna of Egypt, the wife of Thonis, gave to her, for there the land bringeth forth medicines in abundance, and some are good and some are evil."

But in the meantime the Greeks had gathered together a great army and sailed to the land of Troy, that they might avenge themselves on him that had done this wrong. These, having disembarked and pitched their camp, sent ambassadors to Troy and King Menelaüs himself with them, who, when they had come within the walls, demanded of the men of the city both

Queen Helen and the treasure which Paris had carried off. Also they asked that satisfaction should be given for this wrong. To this the men of Troy made answer that they had neither Queen Helen nor the treasure in their city, but that these were in Egypt, and that it was unreasonable to demand from them things that King Proteus of Egypt had in his possession. And this same answer they made both first and last, both as men commonly say such things and also confirming it with an oath. But the Greeks thought they were mocked by the men of Troy. Wherefore they besieged the city until they took it. But when they had taken it and found it was indeed as the men of Troy had said, and that Queen Helen was not there, they sent Menelaüs to Egypt to King Proteus. So Menelaüs departed to Egypt, and sailed up the river as far as the city of Memphis. Then Proteus courteously entreated him, giving him back Queen Helen unharmed and all the treasure with her. Notwithstanding Menelaüs dealt not with the Egyptians as they had dealt with him. For when he would have departed to his own country, and was hindered by contrary winds, and this for many days, he devised a most wicked thing. He took two children of men of the land, and offered them as a burnt-offering. And when this became noised abroad, and there was much indignation against him, he departed in great haste, marching towards the land of Libya. This is the story which the priests of Egypt tell of Menelaüs, and Helen, and Paris. And as for that which concerneth the city of Troy, they say that they heard it from King Menelaüs himself.

When Proteus was dead Rhampsinitus reigned in his stead. This Rhampsinitus had great store of silver, such as none of the kings after him were able to surpass or even to approach. Wishing to keep these riches in safety he would have a treasure-house built, whereof one side was in the outer wall of his palace. But the builder of this treasure-house devised means whereby he should himself have access to it, the means being this: he caused that there should be one stone in the outer wall which could be easily taken from its place by two men, or even by one. So the treasure house was built, and the King laid up his silver therein. Now it came to pass after a time that the builder fell sick, and being about to die called his sons unto him—for the man had two sons—and set forth to them how, not without forethought for them, that they might have stores of wealth without end, he had built the King's treasure-house. Then he made the whole matter plain to them about the taking out of the stone, and gave them the measurements that they might know its place. At the same time he said, "If ye keep this secret, ye shall be stewards after a fashion of the King's treasure." After this the man died, and his sons made no long delay in setting to work, but came by night to the King's palace, and finding the stone in the building, moved it easily from its place, and carried off great store of money. But when the King chanced to open the treasury-house he marvelled to see that the silver was lower in the jars where it was kept. Nor had he whom to blame, for the seals upon the door were not broken, and the door was safely shut. But when the thing happened again, and he found, opening the treasure-house twice or thrice, that the store of silver was diminished—for the thieves ceased not to plunder it—he contrived this thing. He caused men to make nets for hunting, and these he put above the jars in which the silver was stored. Then the thieves made their way into the treasure-house in the same manner as before; but when they came near to the jars, one of them fell into the net that was set for a trap, and was caught. And so soon as the man knew in what an evil plight he was, he called his brother to take counsel with him. To whom he said, "Come hither to me as quickly as thou canst, and cut off my head, lest haply some one should know me and thou perish with me." The man thought that his brother had spoken wisely; therefore he did this thing, and cut off the head of his brother, and departed, carrying off the head, having first fitted the stone in its place.

The next day at dawn King Rhampsinitus, coming into his treasure-house, was beyond measure astonished to see in the trap a body that had not a head, but the house remaining as before, without any place to be seen where a man might come in or go out. Being, therefore, much perplexed, he commanded that they should hang the dead body of the thief from the wall, and over this body he set guards, commanding that if they should see any one weeping or bewailing himself near the place, they should lay hold of the man and bring him before him. Now when the mother of the dead man knew that his body was hung up she was sore troubled, and spake to the son that was yet left to her, commanding him that he should devise means as best he could by which he might carry away the body of his brother. And she affirmed that if he heeded her not, she would go straightway to the King and declare the whole matter, how he had stolen the treasure. Now as the heart of the woman was wholly set upon this thing, and the man for all that he could say could not prevail over her to change her purpose, he contrived this way of doing it. He harnessed asses, and laid on them skins which he had filled with wine, and drave them past the palace. And when he was come to the place where the guards watched the dead body, he loosed the necks of some of the skins. And when the wine ran out abundantly, he made much ado, beating his head with his fist, and crying out aloud, as though he knew not to which of the asses he should first turn. But when the guards saw the wine flow out, they ran into the road, holding pitchers in their hands, thinking to collect some what of it, and so profit by the chance. And at the first the man made as if he were angry, and reviled them; but when they comforted him, he seemed to be persuaded and to abate his wrath. And after a while he drove his asses out of the road as if he would have set their burdens in order. So the guards and he fell to talking and laughing together, and after a while he gave them one of the skins of wine. Whereupon the men lay down as they were, and drank, and would have him bear them company and drink with them. Then the man seemed to be persuaded, and sat down with them; and in time, all being very friendly and merry together, the man gave them another skin, till at the last they had drunk so much that they were wholly overcome, and lay down to sleep in the place. But when the night was now far spent he loosed the body of his brother from the chain wherein it was hung, and for scorn shaved the right cheeks of the guards, and so, laying the body upon the asses, carried it home. Thus did he fulfill that which his mother had commanded him.

But when the King heard that the body of the thief had been stolen, he had great wrath. But being resolved that he would by some means find out the man who had contrived these things, he devised this device. He proclaimed that he would give his daughter in marriage to that man, though he were of the very lowest of the people, who should have done a thing more witty and wicked than any other. So many came wishing to have the King's daughter to wife, and told what they had done. And at last came the thief, for he would not that the King should seem in any way to have outwitted him. And when he was come into the chamber where the King's daughter sat, and she asked him the thing which she had asked of the others, he made answer that the wickedest thing that he had done in his life was this, that he had cut off his brother's head when he had been caught in a trap in the King's treasure-house, but that the wittiest thing was that he had made the King's guards drunk with wine, and so stolen the body of his brother. Now, when the King's daughter heard these things, she stretched forth her hand, thinking to hold him fast, for so it had been commanded her to do. But the man had cut off the arm from a body that was newly dead, and put the arm under his cloak, making as if it were his own. So the King's daughter laid hold of the hand of the dead body, but the thief left it with her, and fled forth by the door. But when they told the King what had befallen, he marvelled beyond measure at the man, so bold was he and so ready of conceit. Wherefore he sent messengers throughout all the towns in his kingdom, saying, that if the man who had done these things would come forth and show himself, he should have free pardon and great rewards to boot, and also that the King would give him his daughter in marriage. And the thief believed that which the King had said, and came forward and showed himself. Whereupon the King did as he had promised, for he said, "The Egyptians surpass all other men in wisdom, but this man surpasseth the Egyptians."

Of this King Rhampsinitus they also tell that being yet alive he went down to the regions of the dead, and played at dice with Demeter, who, they say, is Queen of those parts, and that he sometimes won and sometimes lost, and at the last came back to the earth having a napkin woven with gold, which the goddess had given him for a gift.

Of this journey of Rhampsinitus the Egyptians have yet, they say, this remembrance. On a certain day in the year the priests weave a mantle and bind the eyes of one of their company with a fillet and take him, having the mantle upon him, to the road that leads to the temple of Demeter, and thus leave him, and themselves return. And they say that the priest, having his eyes thus blinded, is led by two wolves to the temple of Demeter, which is distant from the city about the space of two miles and a half, and that also the wolves lead him back from the temple to the place where he was set by his fellows.

CHAPTER XI

OF CERTAIN OTHER
KINGS OF EGYPT

After Rhampsinitus there reigned a certain Cheops; and this king did very wickedly, forbidding the people to do sacrifice to the Gods, and making them labour on certain works which he had set in hand. For it was this Cheops that built the greatest of the pyramids. First he made a causeway, five furlongs long and ten fathoms wide, and in height where it is highest eight fathoms. This causeway was for the carrying of the stones. And these stones were cut from quarries in the Arabian hills, and being drawn to the river were carried across by men appointed for that purpose. And afterwards yet other companies of men drew them to the hills that are on the Libyan side. The number of those that worked was one hundred thousand men, and when they had laboured for three months there came another hundred thousand in their room. The causeway was ten years in building and the pyramid twenty. And when it was finished there was written an inscription on it, saying how much had been spent on radishes, and onions, and garlic for them that built it, and the sum was sixteen hundred talents of silver. How much then must have been the cost of the tools of iron that were used in the work, and of the food and clothing of the men! This Cheops reigned fifty years, and after him, Cephrenes, his brother, reigned fifty years and six months, and behaved himself in the same wicked way, oppressing the people and forbidding to worship the Gods. This Cephrenes also built a pyramid for himself, but it was not equal to the pyramid of his brother.

And when Cephrenes was dead, there reigned the son of King Cheops, Mycerinus by name. This man walked not in the ways of his father, but opened the temples, and eased the people, who were now sorely afflicted by their burdens, that they might go about their own business and do sacrifice to the Gods. Also he gave more righteous judgment in all matters than any of the kings of Egypt before him. And not only did he judge righteously, but if any man, his cause having been tried, was nevertheless not satisfied, he would give him of his own substance, even to the full of his desire. Nevertheless to this Mycerinus, though he dealt gently with his people and was just in all his ways, there happened great calamities. For first of all his daughter died, being his only child. For her, wishing to bury her as none other had ever been buried, he contrived a tomb after this fashion. He made the image of a heifer, of wood and hollow, and gilded it over. In this he buried his daughter, and this was not put into the earth but kept in the temple. And one day in every year they carry it out into the light of day, for they say that the daughter of Mycerinus, when she lay dying, entreated of her father that she might see the sun once in every year. And after the death of his daughter there befell him this second trouble. There came to him an oracle from the city of Buto that he should live six years only, and die in the seventh. Then was the King very wroth, and sent to the god, reproaching him with these words. "My father and my uncle shut the temples, and kept not the Gods in remembrance, and oppressed the people, yet did the Gods give them long life. And lo! because I am righteous, I must die in my youth." But the oracle answered him again, saying, "Thou diest before thy time because thou doest that which thou shouldest not do. For the will of the Gods is that Egypt should be afflicted for one hundred and fifty years. Now the two kings that were before thee knew this thing, but thou knowest it not." When King Mycerinus heard it, knowing that a sentence that should not be changed had gone out against him, he did this. He gave himself up to feasting and all manner of delights, and ceased not either day or night. And that the night might be unto him as the day, he made many lamps, and lighted them so soon as darkness fell upon the earth. And this he did, going from place to place among the woods and wheresoever he heard that there were the pleasantest resorts. Now the reason for which he did this was, that he might show the oracle to have spoken falsely. For this had said that he should live six years only, but he said to himself, "If I live not the days only but the nights also, then shall my years be not six but twelve." This Mycerinus also built a pyramid, but smaller by far than the pyramid of his father.

After Rhampsinitus came King Asychis. In his days there was so great poverty in Egypt that the King made a law that a man might borrow, giving as security the dead body of his father. And if a man paid not the debt, then it should not be lawful to bury him in the tomb of his fathers, or in any tomb whatsoever; and that none of those who were begotten of him should be so buried. This King, wishing to surpass all the kings that had been before him, built a pyramid of brick, with these words written upon it: "Despise me not, when thou lookest at the pyramids of stone, for I surpass these, so much as Zeus surpasseth the other gods. For the King built me thus. When men put poles into the lake, the mud that stuck to the poles they gathered together, and made bricks thereof. So was I built."

AN EGYPTIAN FEAST

After Asychis there reigned a blind man, by name Anysis. In his days Sabacon, King of the Ethiopians, came into Egypt with a great army, and subdued it, and reigned over it for the space of fifty years. But Anysis, the blind King, fled into the marshes, and there made for himself an island of earth and ashes, rising above the waters. For it was so that when one of the Egyptians came to him with food—and this they did without the knowledge of Sabacon—he brought also a gift of earth and ashes. So the island was made. And at the end of fifty years Sabacon dreamed a dream. He saw in his dream a man standing over him and counselling him to gather together all the priests that were in Egypt and cut them asunder. Then King Sabacon judged that the interpretation of the dream was this: that doing some wickedness in holy things he should suffer punishment either from god or man. Therefore he knew that the time was come when he should not reign any more over the land of Egypt. And, indeed, when he was yet in Ethiopia the oracles which the Ethiopians use had told him that he should reign over Egypt fifty years. And now, the time being fulfilled, and the dream troubling him, he departed again of his own accord into the land of Ethiopia.

Next unto Anysis there reigned Sethon, who was a priest of the god Hephæstus. This King held the fighting men of Egypt in no esteem, as thinking that he had no need of them, and, over and above other things, he took away from them the lands which the kings before him had given them. After this it befell that Sanacharibis, King of Arabia and Assyria, came against him with a great army; and the fighting men of the Egyptians would not come to his help. Wherefore, Sethon, the priest, being in a great strait, came into the temple and wept before the image, showing his trouble. And as he wept he dreamed a dream. He saw the god standing

SENNACHERIB IN HIS CHARIOT

over him, and the god bade him be of good heart, for
that he should suffer no harm from the army of the
Arabians, for that he himself would send them that
should help him. Then the King, trusting in these words,
took with him such of the Egyptians as were willing to
follow him, and pitched his camp in Pelusium. Now of
fighting men he had not one, but hucksters only and
handicraftsmen, and such as are found in the market-
place. And when the two armies were encamped over
against one another, there came a great multitude of
field mice into the camp of the Arabians, and devoured
their quivers, and the strings of their bows, and the
handles also of their shields, so that they fled before the
Egyptians, being without arms, and many of them were
slain. For this reason the image of this King stands in
the temple of Hephæstus, having a mouse in his hand,
and this inscription: "Let all men look on me, and
learn to reverence the Gods."

115

When Sethon was dead, the Egyptians set up twelve Kings, for without Kings they could not endure to live, dividing the whole land into twelve parts. These made marriages among themselves, and established it for a law, that none should seek to have more than another, nor do any harm to another, but that they should live in all peace and friendship. Now it had been declared to the twelve Kings when they were first established in their kingdoms, that whosoever of them should pour out a libation from a cup of brass should reign over the whole land of Egypt. And it came to pass that the Kings, having for a long time dealt righteously one with the other, were assembled together in the temple of Hephæstus, for it was their custom to assemble themselves at the temples in order. And on the last day of the feast, when they were about to pour out a libation, the high priest brought out to them cups of gold, for such were they wont to use. But it so chanced that he missed the number, and brought out eleven cups only, there being twelve Kings. Now a certain Psammetichus was one of the twelve. This man, as he chanced on that day to stand last of the twelve, and so had not a cup, took the helmet of brass which he wore upon his head and used it as a cup, pouring out from it a libation. But not he only but all the twelve also had helmets of brass upon their heads. This did Psammetichus without any evil purpose in his mind. But when the other Kings saw the thing which he had done they called to mind the oracle, how it had been foretold to them that he who should pour out a libation from a cup of brass should be King over the whole land of Egypt. Now they thought it not just to slay Psammetichus, having found, when they enquired into the matter, that he had no ill purpose in his heart, but they took from him the most of his power, and banished him into the marshes, and commanded that he should not come forth from the marshes into any part of the land of Egypt. Then Psammetichus, thinking that the eleven Kings had dealt unrighteously with him, bethought him how he might best avenge himself on them. Wherefore he sent to the city of Buto to the oracle of Latona, for this oracle the Egyptians hold to be the most truth-speaking of all the oracles in their land. And the oracle answered him with these words: "Thou shalt have vengeance when there come men of brass from the sea." But Psammetichus could by no means believe that men of brass should come to him as helpers. Notwithstanding, after a while it so chanced that certain men of Ionia and Caria, sailing about to get such plunder as they might light upon, came to the land of Egypt, and disembarked from their ships. These men were clad in armour of brass, and one of the Egyptians seeing them went with all haste to Psammetichus, where he dwelt in the marshes, and told him that men of brass had come from the sea, and were plundering the land, for never before had they seen men clad in such armour. But when Psammetichus heard it, he perceived that the oracle was fulfilled. Wherefore he sent to the men of Ionia and Caria, and made a league of friendship with them, and promising them many and great rewards, sought to persuade them to be on his side. And having persuaded them, he gathered together also such of the Egyptians as favoured him, and using these strangers as helpers, so subdued the eleven Kings. And when he had conquered the whole land of Egypt, he gave to these men of Caria and Ionia places wherein they might dwell. And these places were over against each other, the Nile being between them, and the name of them was the Camps. Also he fulfilled to them all the other promises which he had made. Besides, he put with them certain children of the Egyptians who should learn the Greek tongue; and from them that so learnt it came the interpreters that are in the land of Egypt. This place which they call the Camps is not far from the sea, on that mouth of the Nile which they call the Pelusian; and the men of Ionia and Caria dwelt therein for many years till King Amasis, of whom we shall speak hereafter, took them thence, and removed them to Memphis, where he made of them a body-guard for himself against the Egyptians. This Psammetichus reigned fifty and three years. And of these fifty and three years he was twenty and nine besieging Azotus, which is a great city in the region of Syria, until he took it. Nor was there ever a city which held out so long being besieged as did this city of Azotus.

The son of this Psammetichus was Neco. King Neco was he who sought to make the canal from the Great Sea into the Red Sea, the same that Darius the Persian made again after him. The length of the canal is a four days' sail; and as for its breadth, two three-banked ships of war, being rowed with oars, may pass therein. This canal is filled with water of the Nile. There died in the digging of this canal, in the days of King Neco, one hundred and twenty thousand men. But Neco finished

ASIATICS BRINGING TRIBUTE

it not, but ceased in the midst of his digging, because of an oracle which hindered him, saying, "That which thou doest thou doest for the barbarians." Now the Egyptians call all men barbarians that speak not the same tongue with themselves. But Neco when he had ceased from digging the canal turned his thoughts to battles and wars. And he made ships of war, some to sail on the Great Sea, and others to sail on the Red Sea. These he used when he had need. Also he had an army by land, and fought with the Syrians at Megiddo, and when the Syrians fled before him, he took Cadytis, which is a great city in those parts. And the garment which he chanced to wear when he took it he offered up to Apollo at Branchidæ of the Milesians. When Neco had reigned sixteen years he died, and Psammis his son reigned in his stead.

In the days of King Psammis there came certain men of Elis into Egypt. These men boasted that no men ordered anything more nobly and righteously than they themselves ordered the games in Olympia, and that the Egyptians, for all that they were the wisest of men, could not find out aught by which this ordering might be made better. But when King Psammis heard how these men of Elis were come talking in this fashion, he assembled those that were counted wisest among the Egyptians. Then the Egyptians came together, and enquired of the men of Elis all that it was the custom for them to do in the matter of these games. And the men of Elis told them everything in order, and said that they were come to Egypt to learn whether anything could be added to their ordinances. Then the wise men of Egypt took counsel together, and asked the men of Elis, "Do your own countrymen contend in these games?" And when the men of Elis made answer that it was lawful for their citizens, as indeed for all the Greeks, to contend therein, the Egyptians replied that in making their ordinances they had altogether failed of what was just and right: "For it cannot be," said they, "but that in this matter you will prefer your own citizen when he contendeth in these games, and do wrong to the stranger. If then ye would order them righteously, and are come to Egypt that ye may learn how to do this thing, make this law for your games, that strangers only shall contend therein." This is the answer which the Egyptians made to the men of Elis.

Psammis reigned six years, and in the seventh year he went out to war with the Ethiopians; but died on the way, and Apries his son reigned in his stead. This Apries prospered more than all the kings of Egypt before him save only Psammetichus, his grandfather. He made war with the Sidonians and vanquished them; also he sent his fleet against the fleet of the men of Tyre, who are mighty sailors, and had the upper hand. Thus he prospered for twenty and five years. But when it was ordained that he should be afflicted, evil came upon him in this way. He made war with the men of Cyrene, and was grievously worsted, losing the greater part of his army. And the Egyptians were wroth with him, and rebelled against him, for they said that he had lost these men of set purpose in order that his kingdom might be the more firmly established over the remnant of the people. For which reason such as returned alive from the war and the friends of them that had died rebelled against him. When Apries heard of the matter he sent Amasis, who was one of his captains, to speak with the rebels and persuade them. So Amasis went to them; but as he spake with them, persuading them, a certain man came behind him and put a helmet on his head, crying out that he had crowned him king. And the thing pleased Amasis, for so soon as the rebels had made him king, he made ready to march against Apries. But Apries, when he knew it, sent a certain Patarbemis, who was one of those that waited upon him continually, a man noble and of good repute, and commanded that he take Amasis alive and bring him. But when Patarbemis bade Amasis return with him to the King, the man did but scoff at him in an unseemly fashion. Notwithstanding, Patarbemis was urgent with him that he should obey the King's commandment and come. Whereupon Amasis made answer, "Verily, I have long since purposed to come; nor shall the King have the ordering of my coming, for I will bring many others also with me." And Patarbemis understood the matter; seeing also that Amasis was making ready to march, he departed in all haste, for he would have the King know what had befallen as speedily as might be. But when Apries saw that he returned and brought not Amasis with him, he took no thought, but falling forthwith into a great passion of anger, bade that they should cut off the man's nose and ears. But when the Egyptians that had held with the King saw what had been done, how a man of good repute beyond all others had been shamefully entreated, they also rebelled against the King, and followed Amasis. Then the King armed his hired soldiers, for he had hired soldiers about him, men of Ionia and Caria, thirty thousand in all, and marched against the Egyptians. And the two armies were set in order against each other, near to the city of Momemphis.

And when the battle was joined, the hired soldiers quitted themselves bravely, but nevertheless were worsted, for the Egyptians were more numerous by many times. Thus did Apries fall from his kingdom, from the which he had thought that not even the Gods could cast him down, so did he trust in his strength. And being thus vanquished in battle, he was taken alive and brought to the city of Saïs, to his own house, that was now the palace of King Amasis. And for a while Amasis kept him in the palace, treating him with all honour. But when the Egyptians murmured against him, saying that he did wrong having such respect to one that was his enemy and the enemy of the people, then the King gave up Apries to the Egyptians, and these strangled him. But when he was dead the people buried him in the sepulchres of his fathers. These are in the temple of Athené, hard by the sanctuary, on the left hand of one that entereth the temple. Here also is the tomb of Amasis, but further from the sanctuary, very large and noble, with pillars carved into the likeness of palm-trees, and other sumptuous adornments.

So Amasis reigned over the land of Egypt. And at the first the Egyptians despised him and held him of small account, because he had been one of themselves, and because his house was of little repute in the land. But he brought them over to himself, not indeed by dealing harshly with them, but by his subtlety. He had among his possessions—for he was very rich—a footbath of gold, in which he and his guests were wont to wash their feet before they feasted. This vessel of gold he brake up, and made therefrom an image of a god, and set up this image in that place of the city whither men most resorted. And all the Egyptians, when they heard that an image of gold was set up, visited it and worshipped it greatly. And when King Amasis knew that they thus worshipped it, he called them together, and spake to them, saying, "See now this image, which was of old a footbath and put to unclean uses, but now is greatly worshipped by you all. Know, therefore, that it is with me as it hath been with this gold. For before I was one of you, but now I am your King. Therefore must you do me such honour as is meet for a King." In this manner he brought over the Egyptians so that they served him willingly.

His manner of life was this. He would rise very early in the morning, and would do the business of his kingdom with much zeal and despatch until the time when the market-place begins to fill, which is before noonday. But after this he would drink and make merry with such as sat at talk with him, jesting with them even in unseemly fashion. This his friends took very ill, and counselled him that he should change his ways, saying, "O King, thou dost not well keep thy state and dignity, thus abasing thyself to things common and unseemly. Rather shouldst thou sit in great state upon thy throne throughout the day, and so do the business of thy kingdom. So would the Egyptians know that they are ruled by a great King, and thou wouldst be in better repute. For now thou dost not behave thyself like unto a King." To them King Amasis made this answer: "They that have bows, when they need to use them, bend them, but when they need them not, loose them. For did they bend them always, the bows would be broken. So is it also with a man. If he give himself up to work without ceasing, and indulge not himself on occasion in sport and pastime, it must needs be that madness or disease will come upon him unawares. And because I know this, I do each thing in its season." In these words did King Amasis make answer to his friends when they counselled him.

This Amasis, before he came to the kingdom, was ever a lover of mirth and jesting, and one that cared not to concern himself with serious business. And when he had exhausted his substance, drinking and making merry, he would go about and steal. Then those from whom he had stolen would take him to some oracle, according as one or another might chance to be at hand. And often he was judged to be guilty by the oracle, and often he was acquitted. When therefore he came to the kingdom he did this. To such of the gods as had acquitted him, saying that he was not a thief, he paid no honour, neither sacrificing in their temples nor adorning their shrines with gifts, for he thought that they were not worthy of respect, having lying oracles only. But them that had declared him guilty of theft, these he counted to be true gods, and to have truth-speaking oracles, and held them in great honour.

There was not one of the gods whom he honoured more than Athené, building a gateway for her temple at Saïs of stones very large and fair, and adorning it also with great statues, and with images, of which the forepart was like unto a man, and the hinder part unto a lion. Of the stones some he brought from the quarries of Memphis and others, the mightiest of all, from the island of Elephantiné, which is twenty and two days' sail from Saïs. And of all the marvels in this place there is none greater than this, a chamber hewn out of a single stone. This stone was fetched from Elephantiné. Three years were they in fetching it, and the number of the men that did it was three thousand, pilots all of them. This chamber is twenty and one cubits long, and fourteen broad, and eight high. This is the measure of the chamber from without; and from within it is nineteen cubits or thereabouts, and twelve, and five. This chamber is near the entering in of the temple, for they never brought it into the temple. And the reason why they brought it not in is this, that the architect sighed as it came near to the gate, thinking that the work had been a grievously long time in the doing, and being very weary of it; and that Amasis took this thing for an omen, and would not suffer them to draw it further. But others say that a certain man of those who were moving it with levers was killed at this place, and that for this cause it was not brought into the temple.

BRINGING CORN AND ANIMALS AS TRIBUTE

In the days of King Amasis the wealth of Egypt was greatly increased, for the river gave bountifully to the land, and the land gave bountifully to them that tilled it; and the cities of Egypt were twenty thousand in all. This King made a law for his people, that every man should come year by year to the governor of his province, and show by what means he got his living, and that he who did not so come and show that he lived honestly should be put to death. Solon took this for one of the laws which he gave to the Athenians, borrowing it from the Egyptians. And indeed it is a law which none can blame.

This Amasis was a great lover of the Greeks, giving the city of Naucratis to such as wished to dwell in the land; and to such as would not dwell in it, but traded in it, coming and going, he gave power to build temples and set up altars where they would. For in old times it had not been permitted to foreigners to trade in any place but Naucratis only. Also, when the temple of Delphi was burnt, and the Delphians sought help for the building of it, he gave them a thousand talents of silver. And he made a league and friendship with the city of Cyrene, and married also a woman of Cyrene, Ladice by name. And in many of the Greek cities he made offerings in the temples. This Amasis also subdued Cyprus and made it pay tribute, which none of the kings before him had done.

CHAPTER XII

THE PERSIANS CONQUER EGYPT

CAMBYSES, King of Persia, made war against King Amasis, and led a great army into Egypt, having with him many from the nations which he and his father Cyrus had subdued, and especially Greeks, men of Ionia and Æolia. Now the cause wherefore he made war was this. He sent a herald to King Amasis, demanding that the King should give him his daughter to wife. And this he did by the counsel of a certain Egyptian who had a grudge against King Amasis. And this grudge the man had because the King had chosen him out of all the physicians of Egypt, taking him away by force from his wife and children, to send him to Cyrus, King of Persia, for Cyrus had asked of Amasis that he should send him a physician of the eyes, the most skilful that there was in the land of Egypt. For this cause the man would do King Amasis an injury, and counselled Cambyses that he should ask the King's daughter in marriage. But when the King heard the words of the herald he was in a great strait, for it troubled him to give the maiden to Cambyses, and yet knew not how he should deny her to him, fearing his anger, for the Persians were a mighty people. Yet he would willingly have denied her, for he knew that she would not be a chief wife to Cambyses, for such the Kings of Persia take only from their own people. But at the last he devised this device. There was a daughter of Apries that had been king before him. She only remained alive of the house of Apries; and the maiden was of great stature, and fair exceedingly, and her name was Nitetis. This Nitetis, King Amasis caused to be arrayed in goodly apparel and ornaments of gold, and sent her to Cambyses as if she were his own daughter. And it came to pass after a time when Cambyses would call her by her name that he said to her, "Daughter of Amasis." But when the woman heard these words, she answered, "O my lord the King, Amasis hath deceived thee, and thou knowest it not. For he caused me to be arrayed in royal apparel, and sent me to thee as though I were his daughter. But in truth I was daughter to Apries, whom this man slew, rebelling against his master." When Cambyses heard this, he was very wroth with Amasis, and made war upon him. This is what the Persians say.

But the Egyptians say otherwise. For they would fain make Cambyses to be one of their own nation. Wherefore they affirm that he was the son of this same daughter of Apries, whom she bare to Cyrus. For they say that it was Cyrus that sent the herald to King Amasis, demanding his daughter in marriage. But they speak not the truth in this matter, and moreover know that they speak it not, for the Egyptians have perfect knowledge of the customs of their Persians. Now among the customs is this, that no bastard may be king if there be a true son, and they hold that the children of a woman that is not a Persian, though she be a king's daughter, are bastards. But in truth Cambyses was the son of one Cassandane, that was a woman of the royal house of the Persians. Also the Egyptians tell this story, but neither is this to be believed. One of the women of Persia, coming to the chamber where the wives of King Cyrus were assembled, saw this same Cassandane, and her children standing by her, being very fair and tall. And when she saw them, she fell in great admiration of them, and praised their beauty. But Cassandane said, "Yet though I be the mother of these children, Cyrus holdeth me not in honour, giving my place to a stranger from Egypt." This she said, taking it ill that the King loved Nitetis. And when Cambyses, that was the elder of the two children, heard these words of his mother, he said, "Mother, when I am grown to be a man, I will turn Egypt upside down for thy sake." When Cambyses said this he was ten years old, and the women marvelled at the saying. Nevertheless when he was full grown and had the kingdom of his father, he remembered these words and made war against Egypt.

There is also another thing to be told about this matter. Among the hired soldiers of King Amasis there was a certain man of the city of Halicarnassus, whose name was Phanes. And the man was wise in council and valiant also in battle. This Phanes, thinking that he had suffered some wrong from the King, took ship secretly, and fled from the land of Egypt, desiring to have speech with Cambyses. But as the man was of great account among the hired soldiers, and knew all that concerned the land of Egypt as did none other, King Amasis was exceedingly desirous to take him. Therefore he pursued after him, giving the charge of the matter to one of his ministers whom he judged to be most faithful. And this man, sailing in a three-banked ship, pursued after him, and caught him in the land of Lycia. Nevertheless he brought him not to King Amasis, as he would fain have done, for Phanes prevailed over him by craft, making the guards that should have kept him drunk with wine, and so escaping to the Persians.

And when Cambyses was minded to march into Egypt, but knew not how he should do so, having to cross a great region that was without water, Phanes came to him, and made known to him how things stood with King Amasis, and also how he might best make his march. And his advice was that he should send to the King of the Arabians, and ask of him that he should give him a safe passage through his country, for the only entrance into Egypt is by the desert. And this desert is three days' journey across, in which whole space there was not so much as a drop of water to be found. About this matter there is a thing worth telling. Twice every year wine is brought into Egypt from every part of Greece, and from Phœnicia also; and this wine is in earthen jars. Nevertheless a man will not find even one jar in the whole land of Egypt. And if he would know why this is so, the cause is this. The chief magistrate in each city has a command laid upon him to gather all the jars that are to be found in his own city, and to cause them to be taken to the city of Memphis. And the people of Memphis fill them with water and carry them to the desert parts of Syria. This is done with the jars year after year. But the beginning of this custom was with the Persians, who would thus provide for themselves an easy passage into Egypt; but in the days of King Amasis it was not begun, and the land was yet without water. So Cambyses listened to the counsel of this Phanes of Halicarnassus, and sent messengers to the King of the Arabians, asking that he might have safe passage through his country. This thing the Arabians granted to him, and they pledged their faith the one to the other.

There is no nation in the world that keepeth faith more righteously than do the Persians. And their manner of pledging it is this. When two men would make a covenant between them, there stands another between the two, who cuts with a sharp stone the palm of the hand of each close by the longest of the fingers. After this he taketh a piece from the garment of each, and dippeth the piece in blood, and anoints therewith seven stones that lie between them, calling in the meantime on Dionysus and Urania. After this the man that hath made the covenant commendeth him with whom he hath made it, whether he be stranger or citizen, to all his friends, and these also hold themselves to be bound to him.

Now when the King of the Arabians had made a covenant with the messengers that came to him from Cambyses he did this. He filled with water a great store of camel skins, and loaded the skins on all the live camels that he had in his country, and caused these to be driven into the desert till the army of Cambyses should come. This is the more credible of the stories which are told of this matter; but there is another also, of which, though it be less credible, mention shall be made. There is a great river in Egypt, which men call the Corys, and it flows into the Red Sea. They say that the King of the Arabians caused them to sew together the skins of oxen and of other beasts, and so made a great conduit, which reached over the whole way from the river Corys to the desert, and this is a journey of twelve days. Also in the desert he had great cisterns dug to receive the water. Of these cisterns, they say there were three, and to each its own conduit.

But before Cambyses came into Egypt, King Amasis was dead. Forty and four years had he reigned over the land of Egypt, nor in all that time had there befallen him any great misfortune. And the Egyptians buried him in his own sepulchre, even that which he had made for himself in the temple which he built to Athené, as hath been said before. And Psammenitus his son reigned in his stead. This Psammenitus gathered his army together and pitched his camp in Pelusium, awaiting Cambyses. In his days there happened a great marvel. There fell rain in Thebes, which thing had not been seen before, and hath not been since. But in the days of Psammenitus there fell rain in small drops.

It came to pass when the Persians, having crossed the desert by help of the King of the Arabians, had set their battle in array against the Egyptians, that the hired troops of the Egyptians, being Greeks, and men of Caria, did a very dreadful thing. They were very wroth with

Phanes because he had brought the army of the stranger against Egypt; wherefore they took his children which he had left behind him when he fled, and brought them into the space between the two armies. After this they set up a great bowl, and slew the children, one after the other, over the bowl, before the eyes of their father. And when they had slain all the children they brought water and wine, and poured them into the bowl, and drank therefrom all of them. When they had done this they joined battle with the Persians. And the battle was very fierce, and many were slain on either side, but at the last the Egyptians fled before the Persians.

About them that were slain in this battle there is told a strange thing by the people of the country. The bones of them that were slain lie apart, the Persians by themselves, and the Egyptians by themselves. Now the skulls of the Persians are so thin, that if a man hit them only with a pebble he will break them easily, but the skulls of the Egyptians so strong that scarcely with a great stone will a man break through them. And the people of the country say that the cause of this difference is this that shall be told, and indeed it seems a reasonable thing. An Egyptian hath his head shaved even from a child, and the bone grows thick, the sun beating upon it. But with the Persians it is not so, for they have their heads covered from childhood, wearing turbans and hats.

Now the Egyptians, when they were worsted in the battle, fled without order, and came to Memphis, where they shut themselves within the walls. Then Cambyses sent up the river a ship of Mitylene, having on board a herald, a Persian, who should bid the Egyptians surrender themselves. But when the people saw the ship come to Memphis, the whole multitude of them rushed out of the castle of the city, and destroyed the ship, and tare in pieces all the men that were therein, and carried back the pieces into the castle. Nevertheless, after they had been besieged for a while, they surrendered themselves. So also did the men of Nubia, which borders upon Egypt. This they did without fighting, for they were afraid by reason of what had befallen Egypt. Also the men of Cyrene and the men of Barca, having the same fear, did the like. The gifts from Nubia did King Cambyses receive with favour, but not the gifts of the men of Cyrene. And indeed these sent five hundred pounds of silver only, which seemed to the King too small a present. Wherefore he snatched the money from the envoys, and scattered it with his own hand among the soldiers.

Now, on the tenth day after that he had taken the fort, Cambyses brought Psammenitus, King of Egypt, to a place before the city, to torment him. And Psammenitus had been King for six months and no more. And when Cambyses had set him and others of the Egyptians with him in the place, he made trial what manner of spirit he was of, dealing with him in this fashion. He clothed his daughter in a slave's garments and sent her, carrying a water-pot on her head, to fetch water, sending with her also other maidens, daughters to the chief men of the country. These also were clothed in like manner to the King's daughter. And when the maidens passed before their fathers with much weeping and wailing, then the other princes that had daughters among them that passed by cried aloud and wept, seeing their children in such evil case, but Psammenitus, when he looked and saw what was done, bent only his eyes upon the earth. And when the maidens that bare the water had passed by, Cambyses caused to pass before Psammenitus his son, with two thousand more of the Egyptians that had the same age. All of these had ropes about their necks and bits in their mouths. These were led to execution, that they might be an expiation for the men of Mitylene, whom the Egyptians in Memphis had destroyed together with their ship. For the judges of the King had given this sentence, that for every man that had died in the ship there should die ten of the Egyptians, and these of the chief men of the land. Then the King saw them pass by, and knew that his own son was being led to the place of execution; but, though the other Egyptians that sat about him wept aloud and made much ado, he wept not, but did as he had done about his daughter. And when these had passed by, it fell out that one that had been his companion in past time, a man stricken in years, came by, and the man had lost all his substance, and had nothing save such things as a beggar might have. Being then in such case he passed by Psammenitus and the other princes of Egypt where they sat before the city. And when Psammenitus saw him he wept aloud, and smote his head with his hand, and called to him that had been his companion by name. Now there had been guards set about the King, who watched all that was done by him, and told it to Cambyses. And Cambyses marvelled much at these things, and sent a messenger to Psammenitus, saying, "Thy master, Cambyses, asks thee this. When thou sawest thy daughter in evil case and thy son led by to death, thou didst neither cry aloud nor weep. Why then hadst thou such respect to this beggar, who indeed, for so I hear from others, is nothing akin to thee?" To this Psammenitus made answer, "Know, O son of Cyrus, that the troubles of my own house were greater than that a man could weep for them. But for the trouble of my companion I could weep, when I saw him, how that his grey hairs were brought down from great prosperity to beggary and wretchedness." This answer did he make, and all judged it well said, and the Egyptians say that King Crœsus wept to hear it, for Crœsus had followed Cambyses into Egypt, and that such of the Persians as were present wept also, and that Cambyses himself had some compassion, so that he sent straightway and commanded that the son of Psammenitus should not be slain with the rest of the youths, and also that they should bring the King himself from before the city to his own presence. Now the messengers that were sent found the young man dead already, for indeed he had been slain first of all, but Psammenitus himself they brought to Cambyses. Nor after this did he suffer aught from the Persians, but lived prosperously. And indeed if he had not meddled with dangerous matters he might have had Egypt to rule over, for the Persians are wont to hold the sons of kings in great honour, so that if a king revolt from them, yet they give back his kingdom to his children. This they have often done even to those from whom they have suffered much; for so they restored the kingdom of Inarus the Lybian, who had worked them much mischief, to Thannyras, that was the son of Inarus. Thus might it have been with Psammenitus; only that he sought to draw away the Egyptians from Cambyses, but the matter was discovered and came to the knowledge of Cambyses, wherefore Psammenitus drank bull's blood, and so died.

After this Cambyses came from Memphis to Saïs. And when he was come to Saïs he commanded that they should bring out the dead body of Amasis from the sepulchre wherein he was buried; and when this had been done at his commandment, he bade them scourge it, and pluck out the hair, and prick it with swords, and do to it all kinds of dishonour. All this they did till they were weary, but the body perished not, for that it had been embalmed. And when Cambyses saw this, he bade them burn it, so commanding a most impious thing, for the Persians held that fire is a god. And neither they nor the Egyptians make it a custom to burn their dead. As for the Persians, they do it not for this reason, namely, that they think fire to be a god, as hath been said, and count it unholy to give to him such a thing as a dead corpse for sacrifice. But the Egyptians think that fire is a wild beast, and that this beast devoureth all that it can lay hold of, and that when it has had enough of food it dieth with that that fed it. But they are not wont to give to wild beasts the bodies of them that die; and indeed that they may not be eaten of worms they embalm and so bury them. Therefore when Cambyses commanded this thing, he did that which pleased neither the Persians nor the men of Egypt.

But the Egyptians say that all these things were done not to Amasis but to one of the same age whom they took for Amasis, and that the Persians thought that what they had done to the dead body they had done to Amasis. For their story is that Amasis had asked of an oracle what should happen to him in years to come, and when he heard the things that should befall his own body, he took this man, who chanced to be newly dead, and buried him in the entering in of the sepulchre, and that this man was he whom Cambyses commanded them to scourge, but that Amasis was buried in the back part of the sepulchre. But it is not to be believed that these things were done about the burying of Amasis, but rather that the Egyptians have feigned them.

CHAPTER XIII

CAMBYSES MAKETH WAR UPON THE NATIONS ROUND ABOUT, IS STRICKEN WITH MADNESS, AND SO DIETH

AFTER this, King Cambyses purposed to make war against Carthage, and against the Hammonians, and against the long-lived Ethiopians, the same that dwell in Libya, by the South Sea. And taking counsel about these things, he judged it best to send his ships against Carthage, and to choose out of his army those that should go against the Hammonians, and, as for the long-lived Ethiopians, at the first to send spies into their country. These spies were to see the Table of the Sun, that is said to be in the country of these Ethiopians, whether there be any such table, and they were to spy out other things also; but for a pretence they were to carry gifts to the King of the Ethiopians. Now the Table of the Sun is said to be such as shall now be told. There is a meadow before the city full of all manner of boiled meats of four-footed beasts. On this table, those that are appointed to this office set the meats by night, and by day any one that will comes and takes of the meats. But the people of the country say that the earth produces these things of her own accord. And when Cambyses was purposed to send these spies, he first commanded that there should come to him men from the city of Elephantiné, of the tribe of the Fish-eaters, that knew the tongue of the long-lived Ethiopians. And while these men were coming, he commanded that the ships should sail against Carthage. But the Phœnicians said that they would not sail, for that they were bound by great oaths to the men of Carthage, and that it was a wicked thing for the fathers to fight against their own children. (For Carthage was built by men that went out from the city of Tyre, that is a city of the Phœnicians.) And the King knew that if the Phœnicians would not sail, the rest were of no account. Thus did the men of Carthage escape when the Persians thought to subdue them. For Cambyses judged it not well to constrain the Phœnicians, because they had yielded themselves to him of their own accord, and indeed all the ships of the Persians were manned by Phœnicians.

Now, so soon as the Fish-eaters were come to Cambyses from the city of Elephantiné, he sent them to the country of the Ethiopians, having first commanded them what they should say, and sending also presents by them, a purple robe, and a twisted necklace of gold, and bracelets of gold, and an alabaster box of ointment, and a cask of wine of Phœnicia. Now these Ethiopians to whom Cambyses sent his messengers are said to be taller and fairer than all other men. And the laws that they use are different from the laws of other men. About their kings they have this law, that they choose

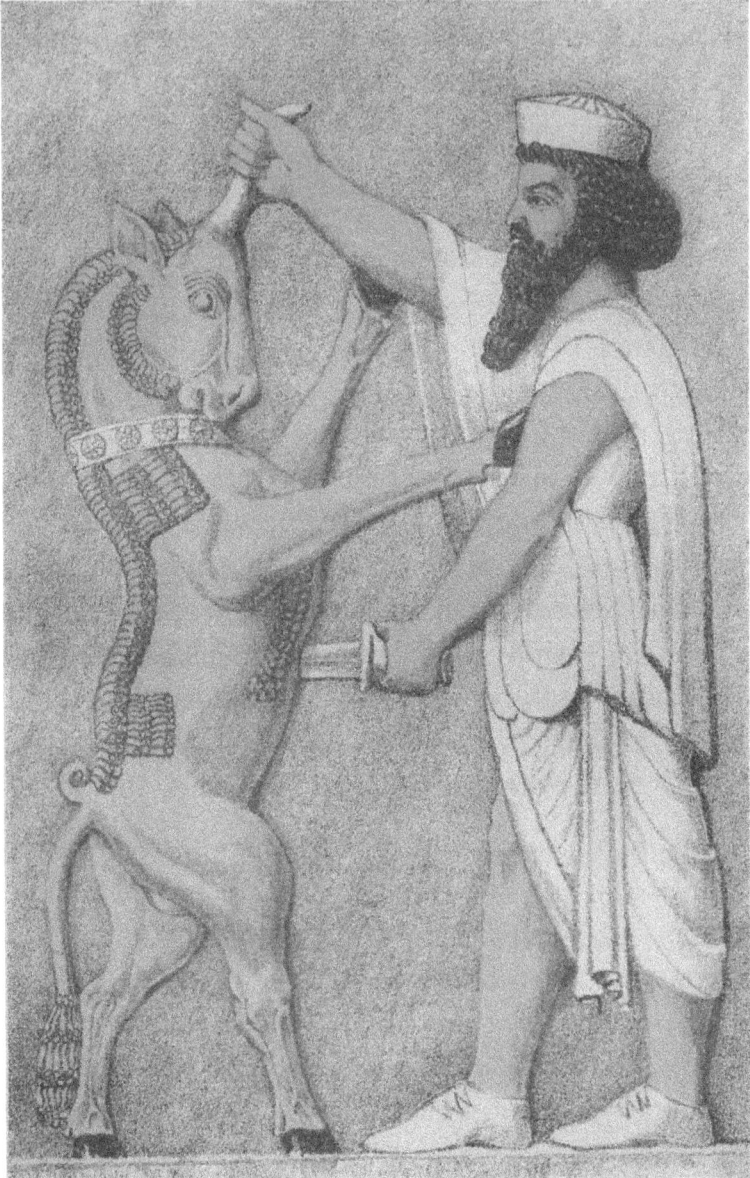

A PERSIAN KING

out from among the citizens him whom they find to be fairest and of greatest stature, and make him their king. To this people, therefore, came the Fish-eaters from Cambyses, and having audience of the King, gave him their presents, and spake, saying, "Cambyses, King of the Persians, would gladly be friend and ally to thee; for which reason he has sent us to talk with thee, and also give thee these gifts, being things in which he himself has his chief delight." But the King of the Ethiopians knew that as spies they were come, and made this answer to them: "The King of the Persians hath not sent you to me because he desired exceedingly to have me for friend and ally, neither have ye said the thing that is true, neither is your King a just man. For indeed had he been a just man, he had not desired to possess any country beside his own, nor to enslave them from whom he hath suffered no wrong. Now, therefore, give ye to him this bow, and speak these words: *The King of the Ethiopians giveth this counsel to the King of the Persians. When the Persian can easily draw this great bow, then let him march against the long-lived Ethiopians; only let him gather a very great army; but till this be so, let him give thanks to the Gods that they have not put it into the hearts of the sons of the Ethiopians to add the lands of others unto their own.*" And when he had so spoken he loosed the bow, and gave it to the messengers. After this he took in his hands the purple robe, and enquired what it was, and in what manner it was wrought. And when the Fish-eaters had told him the truth, that it was of wool and dyed with purple, he said, "These men are full of deceit, and their garments also are deceitful."

143

After this he took in his hand the twisted necklace of gold and the bracelets. And when the Fish-eaters told him that they were for ornaments, he laughed, for he thought them to be fetters, and said, "Nay, but we have in our country stronger fetters than these." Then again he would know about the perfume, and when the men had told him of its making, and how it was used for anointing, he said according as he had about the dye. Last of all he took the wine, and would know how it was made. With this he was pleased beyond measure. After this he enquired of the men what their king had for food, and how many were the years of a man's life among the Persians. To this they answered that the King's food was bread, and set forth to him how bread was made from wheat. As to the years of a man's life, they said that eighty was the full number of them. To this he made answer: "I marvel not at all if your years are so few, when ye have for food that which is but as dung. And I doubt not that as for the years which ye have, ye endure by reason of this most excellent drink." And he put his hand upon the cask of wine, confessing that in this matter the Ethiopians were surpassed by the Persians. Then the Fish-eaters enquired of him what was the manner of life among the Ethiopians, and to what age they commonly came. To this the King made answer that the number of their years was commonly one hundred and twenty, but that some among them over-lived this; and that for food they had boiled meat, and for drink milk. When the men marvelled at this, the King led them to a fountain, in which, when they had washed, they were sleeker than if they had been anointed with oil-olive. The smell of this fountain was as the smell of violets; and so light was the water of it, as the men said, that nothing could float upon it, neither wood, nor things that are lighter than wood, but all things straightway sank. If this water be indeed such as it is said to be, and they use it continually, then is there reason enough why they come to such an age. And when they had seen the fountain, the King took them to the prison, where all the prisoners were bound with chains of gold. Among these Ethiopians there is nothing that is rarer and more precious than bronze. And from the prison they went to see what is called the Table of the Sun. And last of all they saw the sepulchres of the Ethiopians. Now their manner of dealing with the dead is this. They embalm the body, either in the same way as do the Egyptians or in some other; and afterwards cover it with gypsum, and this they paint with colours, so that it is in all points like to the man when he was alive; and having painted it, they put about it a pillar of crystal, made hollow. And this crystal they dig from the earth in great quantity; and it is easily worked. In the middle of this pillar, therefore, may be seen the dead body, nor does it stink at all, or have an unseemly appearance, but is to be seen in all points like to the man when he was yet alive. This pillar the nearest kinsmen of the dead keep for a whole year in their house, offering before it the first-fruits of all things they have, and doing sacrifice to it. And after the year is ended, they take it away and put it in some place near unto the city.

When the messengers had seen all these wonders

they departed again to their homes. But Cambyses, when he heard the words that they brought back from the King of the Ethiopians, fell into a very vehement rage, and set out to march against the Ethiopians, not having made for himself any provision of food, and not considering with himself that he was about to march to the very ends of the earth. But he was as one possessed with madness when he heard the words of the Fish-eaters, and so set forth. The Greeks he commanded to remain in Saïs, where he was, and the rest of the army he took with himself. And when he was come in his march to Thebes, he separated from his army fifty thousand men or thereabouts, and gave commandment to them that they should take the priests of the Hammonians alive and burn the temple of Zeus; but he himself with the rest of the army marched against the Ethiopians. But before he had accomplished even the fifth part of the way, all that they had of food or like to food failed them. And when the food was all spent, then they consumed the beasts of burden. And if Cambyses when he saw these things had considered the matter again, and led back his army to Egypt, he had been a wise man, for all that he had erred at the first. But he took no count of these things, but would still go forward. And indeed while the men could get aught from the earth, they made shift to live, eating grass and the like; but when they came to the sand, then they did a dreadful thing. For each ten cast lots among themselves, and the man on whom the lot fell they devoured. And when Cambyses knew this he was afraid, for it seemed a terrible thing that they should eat each other, and he gave up marching against the Ethiopians, and returned to Thebes, having lost a great part of his army. And from Thebes he went to Memphis, and being at Memphis he let the Greeks that were there depart.

Thus fared the army that marched against the Ethiopians, but as for that which marched against the Hammonians, men know not how it fared. So much indeed men know, that it set out from Thebes, having guides with it, and that it came to the city of Oasis, which is seven days' journey from Thebes across the sand. This Oasis is the same as that which the Greeks call the "Island of the Blest." But as for the things that befell them after this there is known nothing, for they came not to the Hammonians, neither did they return to Thebes. Nevertheless the Hammonians say that when they had left the city of Oasis, and had come to a place which lies midway between the country of the Hammonians and Oasis early in the morning, as they were taking their meat, there came a south wind, very strong and sudden, and blew on them, and that this wind carried with it great columns of sand; and that they were covered with these, and so were seen no more.

About this time befell that which has been told before, how Cambyses wounded to death the sacred bull which the Egyptians call Apis.

The Egyptians say that Cambyses was stricken with madness by reason of his wickedness in doing this thing. But of a truth he had been for some time of an unsound mind. The first of his evil deeds was this, that he slew Smerdis, his own brother. This Smerdis he sent away out of Egypt into Persia on account of envy, because he only was able to draw the bow which the King of the long-lived Ethiopians sent for a gift; and, indeed, Smerdis himself drew it but two fingers' breadth. And when he departed Cambyses saw a vision in his sleep, and the vision was this. It appeared to him as if a messenger came from Persia and told him that Smerdis sat upon the King's throne, and that his head reached even unto the heavens. Wherefore, he feared lest his brother should slay him, and be made king in his stead. For this cause he sent to Persia one Prexaspes, whom he judged to be the most faithful of his servants, and bade him slay Smerdis. And this Prexaspes, having first gone to Susa, did; but whether he slew him when they were hunting together, or took him to the Red Sea and there drowned him, is not certainly known.

Also Cambyses slew one of his sisters. And about her and the manner of her death there are told two tales. For the Greeks say that it befell in this manner. Cambyses, for sport, set a dog whelp to fight with a lion whelp. And when the dog was about to be overcome, his brother brake his chain and helped his brother, and the two together had the mastery of the lion. Now it chanced that Cambyses' sister also saw the thing; and the King was pleased, but the woman wept. And Cambyses asked her why she wept, to which she answered, "I wept because I saw the dog help his brother, for I remembered Smerdis, and know that there is no one to help thee." But the Egyptians say that the woman showed him a lettuce of which she had stripped the leaves, and asked of him whether it were the fairer full or so stripped. And when the King made answer, "The full is fairer," the woman said, "Why then hast thou done to the house of Cyrus as I have done to this lettuce?" Whereupon the King in great anger smote her that she died.

Such madness did Cambyses work against his own kindred, whether on account of that which he did to the god Apis, or of some other thing, such as often befall the sons of men. Some indeed say that from birth he was afflicted with a certain disease of the body; and indeed it is nothing unlikely that he who hath his body diseased should also be diseased in mind.

He did also many frantic things against others of the Persians, as against Prexaspes, of whom mention has before been made. There was none more faithful to him than this Prexaspes, executing all his commands very zealously. Also the King had his son for cupbearer, and this is accounted a great honour. King Cambyses said to this man, "Prexaspes, what manner of man do the Persians hold me to be? And what do they say of me?" To this Prexaspes made answer, "O my lord, as to other things the Persians praise thee greatly, but they say that thou art overmuch given to the love of wine." But when the King had heard this he was very wroth, and said, "The Persians then say that I tarry overlong at the wine, and am not sound of mind. And as to what they were wont in former times to say of me, it is not true." For before this Cambyses had asked of the Persians that sat at meat with him, and of Crœsus, what manner of man they judged him to be in comparison of his father; and they had answered him that he was a better man than his father, for that he had all the possessions of his father, and had gained also in addition both Egypt and the sea. This is what the Persians said, but Crœsus being present was not pleased with their answer, but said this to the King, "As for me, O son of Cyrus, I judge thee not to be equal to thy father, for thou hast not a son, such as he left behind, leaving thee." With this answer of Crœsus Cambyses was beyond measure pleased. Now therefore he remembered the things that had been said to him, and said in great wrath to Prexaspes, "Thou shalt soon learn for thyself whether the Persians speak truly if they thus speak of me, or whether they are rather mad themselves when they say such things. Set thy son yonder in the doorway, and if I shoot at him with an arrow and smite him in the middle of the heart, then shall the Persians be seen to say that which is false, but if I smite him not so as I say, then do the Persians say the truth and I am not of sound mind." When he had said this he drew his bow, and shot at the boy, and hit him. And when the boy fell, the King commanded that they should open the body, and see the wound where it was. And when they found the arrow in the heart of the boy, the King laughed aloud, and was in great joy, and said to the lad's father, "Prexaspes, now is it not manifest that I am not mad, and that the Persians are not of sound mind? And tell me now, didst thou ever see a man shoot so straight at the mark as do I?" To this the man made answer, "My lord, I judge that not even a god could shoot so well." For he saw that the man was mad, and was in fear of his own life. Also Cambyses took twelve men of the Persians, than whom there were none greater in the land, and buried them alive with their heads downward, and this he did for no sufficient cause. But when he did this, Crœsus the Lydian judged it well to give the man counsel, and this he did, saying, "O my lord, it is not fitting that thou shouldst indulge thy heart in all things, rather shouldst thou refrain thyself. For now thou takest men that are of the same nation as thou art and slayest them for no sufficient cause, and thou slayest children also. Take heed therefore lest haply, if thou dost such things, the Persians rebel against thee. And this I say because King Cyrus thy father laid on me a command that I should give thee counsel as I should deem it to be best for thy welfare." This counsel did Crœsus give to Cambyses out of love and kindness. But Cambyses answered him, "Dost thou dare to give counsel to me, having, forsooth, managed the affairs of thine own kingdom excellently well, and having given such excellent good counsel to the King Cyrus my father when thou badest him cross the river Araxes and so fight against the Massagetæ, though these were willing themselves to cross the river and so fight against him? Thou wast an evil ruler to thine own country, bringing it to ruin, and an evil counsellor to the King my father, who perished because he did according to thy word. But verily thou shalt suffer for it, and indeed I have long sought occasion against thee." So saying he laid hold of his bow and would have shot at Crœsus, but Crœsus ran out of the chamber. Then Cambyses, because he could not shoot him, gave commandment to his servants that they should take Crœsus and slay him. But the men, knowing the King's way, slew him not, but hid him away, saying to themselves, "If the King shall repent him of this thing, then will we show Crœsus alive, and receive gifts as the price of his life. But if he shall not repent him, nor feel sorrow for the thing, then will we do the deed." And it befell not many days afterwards that the King repented him of the deed; whereupon the men told him of the thing which they had done, saying that Crœsus was yet alive. Then Cambyses said that it pleased him much that Crœsus was alive; but as for the men, that he would not give them any reward, but would slay them. And this he did.

For these and many other things which he did it is manifest that King Cambyses was not of a sound mind; especially because he scoffed at sacred things, making sport of the images of the Gods, and intruding himself into holy places into which it is not lawful but for the priests to enter. For indeed there is nothing that all men hold more sacred than custom. And if a man were to give all nations the choice of the best customs which they could find in all the earth, assuredly each nation would choose its own customs. It is therefore not to be believed that a man should scoff at such things, except indeed he were mad. But that it is true as hath been said, that men hold the custom which they themselves follow to be the best, may be proved by many proofs, and not the least clearly from that which shall now be told. Darius, King of Persia, having called for certain Greeks that were about his court, asked them for how great a sum of money they would eat their fathers when they should die; and the Greeks answered that for no sum of money whatsoever would they do such a thing. After this Darius called certain Indians before him. Now these Indians eat their parents when they are dead. The King therefore asked them, the Greeks being present, and understanding by means of an interpreter the things that were said, for how great a sum of money they would be willing to burn their fathers with fire when they should die. But these men when they heard it cried aloud, saying that he should not speak of such horrible doings. Wherefore it seems that Pindar spake well when he said, "Custom is the king of all."

Now it came to pass that, Cambyses tarrying long time in Egypt, and plainly showing himself to be mad, there rebelled against him two Magians that were brothers; and one of these two Cambyses had left to be steward of his house. Now this man knew that Smerdis had been slain, and that the matter had been kept secret, and that the Persians that knew it were few in number, the most part supposing that the man was yet alive. Knowing this, therefore, he contrived a plot by which he might possess the kingdom. He had a brother, the same that joined him in his rebellion, and the name of this brother was Smerdis, and he was very like in face to Smerdis the son of Cyrus, that had been slain by his brother King Cambyses. Very like was he in face, and he was of the same name also. The elder of the two, therefore, having assured the other that he would accomplish the whole matter for him, set him on the throne. And when he had done this, he sent heralds to the provinces, and a herald also to Egypt, bidding him proclaim to the army that they should thereafter follow Smerdis the son of Cyrus, and not Cambyses any more.

All the other heralds did as it had been commanded them, and so did the herald that was sent to Egypt. This man found Cambyses and his army in Agbatana, which is a town of Syria, and going into the midst of the host, stood before them all, and proclaimed with a loud voice the words which the Magian had told him. And when Cambyses heard the words of the herald, thinking that they were true words, and that he had been deceived by Prexaspes, who having been sent to slay Smerdis had not slain him, he looked at Prexaspes, and said to him, "Prexaspes, is it thus that thou didst the business that I committed to thee?" Then Prexaspes made answer, "O my lord, these words are not true, nor hath thy brother Smerdis rebelled against thee, nor shalt thou ever have any quarrel with him, be it great or small. For indeed I did the thing which thou commandedst me, and buried the man with my own hands. But if the dead rise, then indeed thou mayest look for Astyages the Median to rebel against thee. But if it be with the dead as it hath ever been, then from that man thou shalt never have trouble. Do thou, therefore, send men to follow after this herald, and overtake him, and ask thou him from whence he cometh, bidding us obey King Smerdis." Then the thing which Prexaspes said pleased Cambyses, and he sent men to bring back the herald. And when the man was returned, Prexaspes enquired of him, saying, "Man, thou sayest that thou art come as a messenger from Smerdis, the son of Cyrus. Tell me therefore this one thing only, and so depart in peace. Didst thou see Smerdis face to face when he gave thee commandment to say these words, or didst thou hear them from one of his servants?" And the man made answer, "I have never seen Smerdis, the son of Cyrus, from the day that King Cambyses marched into Egypt. But the Magian whom Cambyses made steward of his household, he it was that commanded me to say these words to you." The man spake thus, hiding nothing of the truth. Then said King Cambyses, "Prexaspes, thou hast been a good servant to me, doing the thing which I commanded thee. But tell me, who of the Persians hath rebelled against me, taking to himself the name of Smerdis?" Then Prexaspes answered, "My lord the King, I understand the whole matter. They that have rebelled against thee are the Magians, Patizeithes, whom thou madest steward of thy household, and Smerdis his brother." But when Cambyses heard these words and the name of Smerdis he was struck to the heart, thinking of his dream and of the interpretation of it, how that he had seen one who told him that Smerdis sat upon the throne, and that his head reached unto the sky. And when he knew that he had slain his brother for nought, he wept for him and bewailed him. But when he had finished weeping, great anger possessed him, and he leapt upon his horse, having it in his mind to march as speedily as might be to Susa against the Magians. But as he leapt upon his horse, the leather of the sheath of his sword fell off, and the sword being thus bared wounded him in the thigh, and the place of the wound was the same, it was said, in which he had wounded the god Apis. Then Cambyses, judging that he was wounded to the death, asked them that were about him, "What is the name of this city?" And they

155

answered him, "The name of this city is Agbatana." Now it had been declared to Cambyses by the oracle of Buto in Egypt that he should die in Agbatana. And Cambyses had thought that he should die when he should have come to old age in Agbatana that is in Media, but the oracle spake of Agbatana in Syria. And when he heard the name of the city, then, being sore troubled by that which he had heard of the Magian, and by his wound also, he came back to a sound mind. Therefore, understanding the oracle, he said, "Here is it decreed that Cambyses the son of Cyrus shall die." More indeed he spake not at that time, but twenty days afterwards he called together the most considerable of the Persians that were with him, and spake to them according to these words: "Men of Persia, there is laid upon me this burden to make known to you the thing which of all things I most desired to hide from you. For when I was in the land of Egypt I saw in my sleep such a vision as it had been well for me never to have seen. I saw a messenger coming to me from home, and saying, 'Smerdis sitteth on the King's throne, and his head reacheth unto the heavens.' Fearing, therefore, lest my brother should take my kingdom from me, I did a thing that was hasty rather than wise. For, indeed, it is not possible for a man to turn away from him that which is ordained, yet did I, being a fool, send Prexaspes to Susa, that he might slay Smerdis. And having done this great wickedness, I lived without fear, not thinking that some other Smerdis might rise against me. And because I knew not that which should come to pass, I made myself the murderer of my brother, and served no end thereby, for lo! I am not the less robbed this day of my kingdom. For the Smerdis that I saw in my dream to rebel against me is this Magian. But now the deed is done. Be ye sure, therefore, that Smerdis the son of Cyrus ye shall see no more; and that they who possess the kingdom are the Magians, to wit, the man whom I made to be steward of my household, and Smerdis his brother. And now he who should by right have avenged me of these men from whom I suffer this wrong is dead, having been slain by the hand of him that was nearest to him. Wherefore, he being thus dead, it only remains for me to tell you, ye men of Persia, that which I would have you do, when I also am departed. For I lay this charge upon you by all the gods of our royal house, and specially upon you that are of the lineage of Achæmenes, that ye suffer not the kingdom to pass from you to the Medes. And if they have taken it by craft, then I charge you that ye take it from them again by craft; and if they have mastered it by strength, then that by strength ye also recover it again. And if ye so do, then I pray that your land may bear its increase for you, and that your wives bear you children, and your flocks and herds be multiplied, and that you be free men for ever. But if ye do not recover it, or at the least, do your utmost at recovering it, then I pray that all things contrary to these may befall you, and moreover, that every one of you, as many Persians as there are, may perish, even as I perish this day." And when he had so spoken, Cambyses lifted up his voice and wept, bewailing himself and his evil lot. And when the Persians saw that the King bewailed himself, they rent their garments, every one of them, and cried in a most lamentable fashion. And not a long while afterwards, the bone breaking away and the flesh of his thigh mortifying, Cambyses the son of Cyrus died, having reigned in all seven years and six months. And he left no issue, neither male nor female. There remained, therefore, of the house of Cyrus one daughter only, Atossa by name.

CHAPTER XIV

THE FALSE SMERDIS IS SLAIN

Now the Persians believed not the words of Cambyses that the kingdom was in the hands of the Magians, thinking that he had said these things for envy and hatred of Smerdis, to the end that the Persians might be made enemies to him. Prexaspes also was very vehement in denying that he had slain the true Smerdis, for indeed he would have been in great peril of his life, now that Cambyses was dead, confessing that he had slain a son of Cyrus with his own hand. Wherefore the Magian reigned in peace, feigning that he was Smerdis the son of Cyrus. And this he did for seven months, during which time he showed great kindness to all the nations over which the kings of Persia rule, so that when he was overthrown all Asia lamented for him, and the Persians only rejoiced. For indeed he sent to every nation and proclaimed that for the space of three years they should neither bear arms nor pay tribute. This proclamation he made at the beginning of his reign, but in the eighth month he was overthrown. And the manner of his overthrowing was this.

There was a certain Otanes among the Persians,

159

that was both well born and rich, so that none other of the people excelled him in these respects. He it was that first had the thought that the Magian, whoever he might be, was not of a truth Smerdis the son of Cyrus; and the reason of his thought was this, that the man never came forth from the castle, and admitted not any of the great men among the Persians to his presence. Having therefore this thought he did thus. He had a daughter, Phœdime by name, that had been married to Cambyses. Now the Magian had taken this Phœdime and the other wives of Cambyses to be his wives. Therefore Otanes sent to his daughter, saying, "Who is this man that is thy husband? Is it of truth Smerdis the son of Cyrus or some other man?" And the woman answered, "I know not, for Smerdis the son of Cyrus I never saw, and I know not who is this man." Then Otanes sent again, saying, "If thou knowest not Smerdis the son of Cyrus yet doth Atossa know. Enquire therefore of her." For Atossa was the daughter of Cyrus. But Phœdime sent to her father, saying, "I cannot come to speak with Atossa, or with any of the women that dwell in the palace. For so soon as this man, whoever he be, came to the kingdom, he ordered it thus with the women in the palace, that they should not have speech the one with the other." But when Otanes heard this it was manifest to him that the matter was indeed as he had thought. Therefore he sent to his daughter a third time, saying, "My daughter, thou art come of a good stock, and shouldst not shrink from such task as thy father shall set thee, though it be full of peril. If this man be not Smerdis the son of Cyrus, but he whom

I think him to be, surely he shall not go unpunished, taking thee to wife, and sitting upon the throne of the Persians. Do thou therefore after my words. When the man is asleep, touch his ears; and if thou find that he hath ears, then know that thy husband is Smerdis, the son of Cyrus, but if he hath them not, that he is Smerdis the Magian." Then Phœdime sent to her father, saying, "This truly is a perilous task thou settest me. For if the man have not ears and I be found touching him in this fashion, without doubt he will slay me. Nevertheless, I will adventure it." Now Cambyses had cut off the ears of Smerdis the Magian for some great crime. So when the time came, Phœdime felt the head of the man, and knew that he had no ears. And so soon as it was day, she sent to her father, and told him the truth.

So soon as Otanes heard this he took to him two other of the Persians, Aspathines and Gobryas, princes both of them, and friends to himself, and set forth the whole matter to them. These men had already the same thought about it as had Otanes; and when they heard what he said, they listened to him readily. Then it seemed good to the three, that they should each choose the man whom he judged to be most faithful and steadfast. And Otanes chose Intaphernes, and Gobryas Megabyzus, and Aspathines Hydarnes. And there being now six of them, there came to Susa Darius the son of Hystaspes from Persia, of which province his father was the governor. And it seemed good to the six to take this Darius to them. So these seven men sware to each other that they would keep faith, and so consulted together. And when it came to Darius to declare his sentence, he said, "I thought that I, and none other, knew that the Magian was king, and that Smerdis the son of Cyrus was dead. And indeed I came to Susa in all haste for this very purpose, to contrive that this man should be slain. And now, since ye know the matter also and not I only, my judgment is that we should do the thing speedily and make no delay. For in such a matter it is not well to delay." To this Otanes made reply: "Son of Hystaspes, a valiant man is thy father, and thou art like to prove thyself as good as he. But as to this matter, be not hasty and rash, but deal as prudently with it as may be. And first there must be more of us before we put our hands to it." Then said Darius: "Hearken to me ye that are present. Be ye sure that if ye follow the counsel of Otanes ye will perish miserably, for some one will carry the matter to the Magian, hoping thus to gain advantage for himself. Rather should ye have kept the matter to yourselves, and done the deed without delay. But now, since it hath seemed good to you to make it known to others, and ye have also opened it to me, I say this. Let us do the deed this very day; or verily, if this day pass by and it be not done, I will go before any other, and tell the whole matter to the Magian." To this Otanes made answer: "Come then, since thou wilt have us make haste, and wilt not suffer us to delay, say by what means we may make our way into the palace, for that guards are set about it everywhere thou knowest, having seen them thyself, or, at the least, heard of them. How shall we pass these by?" Darius answered, "There are many things, Otanes, which cannot be shown by words but by deeds only; and many things also which have a fair look when one speaketh of them, yet doth nothing good come of them. As for these guards that are set about the palace, ye yourselves know that it is in no wise difficult to pass them by. For first there is no man of them who, knowing what place we have in this kingdom, will stay us from passing, such reverence, nay, such fear will he have of us; and next, I myself have a most excellent pretence by which I will pass, for I will say that I am lately come from the province of Persia, and that I have a message from my father to the King. And indeed, when a lie is needed, then let a man lie. For they that lie and they that speak the truth seek the selfsame thing. They that lie, lie because they hope by persuading another to gain some advantage for themselves, and they that speak the truth, speak it desiring so to get some gain to themselves, being the better trusted in time to come. Thus, though they follow not in the same way, they seek the same end. And surely, if they were like to get no gain in the matter, then would the speaker of truth become a liar, and the liar a speaker of truth. But as to these guards, whosoever shall let us pass of his own free will, it shall be the better for him in time to come; and whosoever shall seek to hinder us, he shall be counted for an enemy. Him will we thrust aside, and so entering do our business." Then said Gobryas: "My friends, we shall never have fairer chance than this to win back the throne; or, if we fail to win it, then to die. For now we, who are Persians, are ruled by a Mede, and this a Magian, and one, to boot, that hath no ears. As for you that were with Cambyses when he was sick, do ye not remember how, being now about to die, he denounced all manner of evil against you, if ye sought not to recover the kingdom? Then indeed we counted not his words to be true, thinking that he spoke from jealousy of his brother; but now have we proof of them. Wherefore I give my vote for this, that when we break up this assembly of ours we go forthwith against the Magian to slay him.

Now, while these seven men were thus holding counsel together, there fell out other things which shall now be told. It seemed good to the two Magians to make Prexaspes their friend; and this they did because they knew that he had suffered a great wrong at the hands of Cambyses, who had slain his son by shooting at him, and because he alone among the Persians knew for a certainty that Smerdis the son of Cyrus was dead, having indeed slain him with his own hand, and also because Prexaspes was held in high repute among the Persians. Wherefore they called him to them and sought to make him their friend, binding him by pledges and oaths that he would keep to himself and not disclose to any man the deceit which they had devised against the Persians, and they on their part promised that they would bestow on him all manner of good things. And Prexaspes promised to do as they would have him. Thereupon they said that they would gather together all the Persians to the royal castle; and they bade him go up on a high tower that was in the castle, and proclaim to the men that their King was Smerdis the son of Cyrus, and none other. This commandment they gave him, knowing that he had been shamefully entreated by Cambyses, and because there was no man whom the Persians would be more willing to believe than this Prexaspes, and also because he had often and vehemently affirmed that Smerdis the son of Cyrus was yet alive, and had denied that he had himself slain him. And when Prexaspes had said that he was ready to do all this, then the Magians assembled all the Persians at the royal castle, and set Prexaspes on a high tower, and bade him say on. But the man said not a single thing of that which they had commanded him, but set forth the genealogy of Cyrus, beginning with Achæmenes, and when he came to Cyrus himself, he related all the good which he had done to his people; and when he had ended speaking of this, he told the whole truth about the matter in hand, saying that he had before concealed it, as knowing that it would not be safe for him to speak the truth, but now, he said, there was a strong necessity laid upon him to unfold the whole matter. So he told the Persians how, under compulsion from Cambyses, he had himself slain Smerdis the son of Cyrus, and how the Magian was king of the realm. Also he called down many curses on the Persians if they did not recover the kingdom for the Persians, and so avenge themselves on the Magians. And having said so much, he threw himself down with his head foremost from the tower, and so died.

But the seven Persians, having resolved as hath been before told, to do their business at once and make no delay, prayed to the Gods, and so departed, knowing nothing of that which had befallen in the matter of Prexaspes. But when they were on the way, having now performed the half of the journey, they heard what had befallen. And when they heard it, they stood aside out of the way for a while, and held counsel with themselves. Then Otanes and they that were with him advised that they should by all means defer the matter, neither adventure themselves when all things were in such tumult; but Darius and his friends were urgent that they should finish it forthwith and make no delay. And while they disputed, they saw seven pairs of hawks that were pursuing two pairs of vultures, and tearing them with their claws and picking them with their bills. And the seven when they saw this sight took heart, and assented all of them to the counsel of Darius, and went straightway to the palace. And when they were come to the gates, then it fell out even as Darius had said, for the guards had respect to the seven, knowing them to be princes among the Persians, and not thinking, indeed, that they had any ill purpose, and so let them pass, and it seemed as if the Gods themselves led them to their work, for no one asked them any question. And when they had passed the guards and were come into the hall of the palace, there met them certain of the eunuchs that are wont to carry messages for the King. These enquired of them for what purpose they had come, and blamed the keepers of the door that they had suffered them to pass, and sought to hinder them that they should not go further. Then the seven encouraged one another, and drew their daggers and stabbed those that would have stopped them, making their way with all haste into the chamber of the men. Now it chanced that both the Magians were within, holding counsel about the matter of Prexaspes, what it were best for them to do. And when they perceived that there was a stir among the eunuchs and also heard them cry out, they themselves ran forth, for they would fain know what had happened. And so soon as they knew it, they sought to defend themselves, and one of them laid hold of a bow and the other of a spear. And when they had done this the seven closed with them. Now he that had the bow and arrows found them of no avail, for his enemies were upon him, neither could he use them. But he that had the spear did somewhat with it, for he wounded Aspathines in the thigh, and Intaphernes in the eye. As for Intaphernes he died not of his wound, but the sight of his eye was destroyed. Then the other Magian, he that had the bow and arrows, seeing that they availed him nothing, turned and fled into an inner chamber, for there chanced to be such hard by the chamber where they were; and two of the seven, to wit Darius and Gobryas, followed hard upon him and entered also. And as Gobryas laid hold on the Magian and rolled with him on the ground, Darius stood over them, not knowing what he should do, for it was dark, and he feared lest he should smite Gobryas. And when Gobryas saw that he stood and did nothing, he cried to him, "Why dost thou not strike?" And Darius answered, "I am afraid lest I should smite thee." Then said Gobryas again, "Let drive with thy sword, though it be through the two of us." And Darius hearkened, and let drive with his sword, and, as it chanced, slew the Magian.

And when they had slain the two Magians, and had cut off their heads, they left the two that were wounded, for these had not strength to follow them and might also serve to keep the castle, and rushed forth, holding the heads of the two Magians in their hands, and called to the other Persians, to whom also they told the thing which they had done and showed the heads. And while they did this they slew any Magian whom they chanced to meet. Then the other Persians, when they knew what had been done, and how they had been deceived of the Magians, thought it well to do likewise, and drew their daggers and slew all the Magians whom they found. And indeed they had not left any Magian alive, only that the darkness stopped them in their deed. This day the Persians keep ever in remembrance, and hold a great feast upon it, calling it the "Massacre of the Magians." And on that day no Magian may come forth, but they all keep themselves in their houses.

Now, after four days, when the tumult had now ceased, the seven met to take counsel concerning the affairs of the kingdom. And first they discoursed as to what manner of government it would be best to establish. Then Otanes set forth his opinion that it would be well to give the power to the whole nation. "For consider," he said, "what oppression ye endured from Cambyses, and of late also from this Magian. For even a good man, if he be not bound to answer for his doings, hath his heart lifted up in him, and is led astray to do all manner of violence and wrong, and to shed innocent blood. But if the people bear rule, then every man answereth for his doings, and all have right and justice." To this Megabyzus made answer: "I like not more than doth Otanes the rule of one man; but I agree not with him when he seeketh to give power to the multitude. For if the oppression of one man be hard to bear, how much less to be endured is that which a man suffereth from the multitude! For the one knoweth the thing that he doeth, but the other knoweth not anything. My counsel, therefore, is that we choose out a company of the wisest men of the nation, and commit the government unto them." Last of all Darius said: "I hold with that which Megabyzus hath said of the multitude; but with that which he hath said of the few I hold not. For I count nothing to be better than the rule of one man. And indeed if the government be with the few that are accounted wise then arises strife between them, and from strife civil war, and at last one ruler is set up. And as for the multitude, though there be not strife, yet no man thinketh but of his own gain. And here also at the last one man is wont to stand up and set right that which hath been ill done; and so do things come round to the rule of one. For which reasons, and because it is not well to change the customs of our forefathers, I give my vote that we commit the government to one man."

Now when Darius had thus spoken, four out of the seven declared themselves to be of the same opinion. Then Otanes, seeing that he could not prevail, said this: "I perceive that it must needs be that we set up one of us to be a king, either casting lots or giving the choice to the Persians that they should elect whom they will, or by some other means. Now in this strife I take no part. I wish not to rule or to be ruled. Therefore I stand apart from the whole matter on this condition, that I be not subject to any of you, neither I, nor my children, nor my children's children after you." To these words they all agreed. So Otanes contended not for the kingdom, but stood apart. And to this day his house only of the whole nation of the Persians is free, being subject so far only as it will, but not transgressing the laws of the realm.

After this the seven took counsel together how they might best choose one of them to be king. And first they determined that to Otanes and to his children for ever, if the kingdom should fall to another than he, there should be given year by year a Median robe and such other gifts as are counted to be most honourable among the Persians. And this they did because Otanes first devised the whole matter, and set them upon slaying the Magian. This then they gave to Otanes for himself; and to the others of the seven, that it should be lawful for them at all times to have audience of the King, and that without announcement made. Also they deemed that it should not be lawful for the King, whoever he might be, to take to himself a wife, except from the families of the seven. And as to the kingdom, they agreed among themselves upon this sign, that they should all ride together before the city the next morning, and that he should be king whose horse should first neigh. Now Darius had for a groom a cunning fellow, whose name was Œbares. This man had a device by which he could make a horse neigh; and this he did the next morning when the seven rode together before the city. And it also befell that when the horse of Darius neighed there came lightning and thunder from a clear sky. And when the five others saw this they leaped from their horses, and did obeisance to Darius.

Thus was Darius the son of Hystaspes made King of the Persians.

CHAPTER XV

THE KINGDOM OF DARIUS

WHEN Darius was established in his kingdom he divided it into twenty provinces, and set rulers in each, calling them satraps. And to each province he appointed a set tribute, either of gold or silver; for before his days, when Cyrus was king, and afterwards in the days of Cambyses, there was no set tribute, but the nations brought gifts to the King. For this reason the Persians were wont to say that Darius was a trader, and Cambyses a master, and Cyrus a father; for that Darius made a trade of everything, and Cambyses was violent and harsh, but that Cyrus was gentle as a father is gentle to his children, and devised for his people all manner of good things.

Darius ruled over all Asia, only that the Arabians were not subject to him but friends; and indeed, but for their friendship, the Persians had not conquered Egypt. Nevertheless they brought gifts to the King, a thousand talents of frankincense by the year. The other nations brought a tribute of gold or silver according to their power. But the people of Cilicia brought also three hundred and sixty white horses, one for every day in the year. And the manner of the King with his tribute is this.

He causeth it to be melted down; and when it is melted it is poured into earthen vessels, which being broken away there remains a mass of gold or silver. And if the King need money he takes as much as he will, and it is coined. But of all the nations there is none that payeth more tribute than the Indians, for these furnish three hundred and sixty talents of gold dust by the year.

Of these Indians there are many strange things to be told. There is a tribe among them called the Padæans that has this custom. If one of them be sick, either man or woman, they deal with him after this fashion. The man's friends come together to kill him, saying that if he be suffered to pine and waste away with sickness, his flesh will suffer damage. And though the man protest most vehemently that he is by no means sick, they pay no heed to his words, but slay him and make a feast of his flesh. And if it be a woman that is sick, then the women that commonly consort with her deal with her in the same way. And if it so chance that any one live to old age, him they sacrifice to the Gods and so devour. But of these there are but few, seeing that every one that falleth into any kind of disease is slain. Other Indians there are that will kill no manner of living creature. These live on a seed that groweth in their country of about the bigness of millet.

The Indians that gather the gold are the most warlike of all; and the way of gathering it is this. There is near to this people a sandy desert, and in this desert dwell great ants, somewhat smaller of size than dogs but bigger than foxes. (The Persian King keepeth some of these ants which the hunters have caught for him.)

These ants make their dwellings by burrowing under the earth in the same manner as do the ants in Greece, to which indeed they are very much like in shape. Now the sand which they throw up is full of gold. The Indians therefore go into the desert after this sand, each man having with him three camels, yoked together side by side, a she-camel in the middle and a male camel on either side. The man rides on the she-camel and chooseth for himself one that has at home a young foal. Now the she-camels are as swift to run as horses, and for the bearing of burdens much better.

When the Indians have thus equipped themselves, they set out to seek for the gold. And they so order the time of their going that the time of seeking may be that when the day is at its hottest, for then the ants hide themselves in the sand by reason of the heat. And in these lands the sun is hottest in the morning, and not as he is wont to be elsewhere, at noon, but rather from his rising to the time of the closing of the market. Then indeed he scorcheth more furiously than he doth in Greece at the noonday, so that the men of that country are fain, it is said, to drench themselves with water. But at midday he burns the Indians as much and no more than he doth other men. But in the afternoon the heat is as the heat of the morning elsewhere, and at sunset there is great cold. So soon as the Indians are come to the gold country, they fill with sand the wallets which they have with them, and so depart with all the speed they may. For the ants find out their coming by the smell, and pursue. And these creatures, say the Persians, are swifter than anything else in the world; nor would any of the Indians escape but that that they are already far upon their way before that the ants have gathered themselves together. And they say that in the flight the male camels, which indeed are not so fleet of foot as the she-camels, begin to drag behind both the one and the other, but the she-camels never slacken their speed one wit, for they remember the young ones which they have left behind them. Thus do the Indians get the most part of their gold, but some they dig out of the earth, only of this there is no great plenty.

A LION HUNT

Such countries as are at the ends of the world bear all things, it would seem, of the very best and largest, even as Greece, which is in the centre of the world, has its seasons most excellently well tempered. So in India, which lieth more to the east than all other countries, the four-footed beasts and the birds are bigger than may be seen elsewhere. Here also there is much gold, of which some is dug from the earth, and some washed down by the rivers, and some, as has been said, stolen from the ants. Also there is in this country a tree which hath a fruit like unto wool; from the fruit of which tree the Indians make their garments.

Arabia lieth farther to the south than all other lands; and in this land only are found frankincense, and cassia, and cinnamon. All these spices the Arabians get not without much trouble and danger; for the trees on which the frankincense grows are guarded by flying serpents, of which there is a great multitude round about each tree. These are small and of various colours; and they drive them from the trees by burning the gum styrax beneath them.

As to the cassia, they gather it thus: they cover their whole bodies and faces with ox-hide and other skins, but the eyes they leave uncovered, and so go seeking the cassia. Now this cassia groweth in a lake, and the lake is not deep, but about it dwell certain winged beasts, very like to bats. These screech in horrible fashion and are fierce exceedingly, and the men keep them from their eyes, and so gather the cassia.

But as to the gathering of the cinnamon, there is something yet more wonderful to be told. For where it groweth and what manner of country beareth it they know not. But they affirm, though the thing indeed is scarcely to be believed, that it groweth in the same land in which Bacchus was reared. The Arabians say that great birds carry the sticks (which the Greeks call cinnamon, having learnt this word from the Phœnicians) for the building of their nests, and that these nests are fastened with mud to the face of cliffs that are very steep and such as a man can by no means approach. But the Arabians devise this way of getting the sticks. They cut up the oxen and asses and other beasts that die in their land into pieces as great as may be, and carry these pieces of flesh to the country of the cinnamon, and having laid them down near to the cliffs, so depart. Then the birds fly down and lay hold of the pieces of flesh, and carry them up to their nests; but these, not being able to bear the weight, are broken down and come to the earth. Then the men return and gather the sticks of cinnamon, and send it out to other countries.

So many are the spices that grow in this land of Arabia that the whole country hath a marvellously sweet smell. It hath also two strange kinds of sheep, such as are not to be found elsewhere. The one kind have long tails, three cubits long at the least. And that these tails may not get wounded, as indeed they would were they dragged along upon the earth, the shepherds do so much carpenter's work as to make trucks for the tails. The tails are put upon trucks, each sheep having a truck for himself. The other kind have their tails very broad, even to the breadth of a cubit.

There is a plain in the land of Asia that is shut in with mountains on every side, but through the mountains there are five passes. This plain once belonged to the Chorasmians, but since the Persians have had the rule of Asia it hath belonged to the Great King. Now from the mountains wherewith this plain is shut in there floweth a great river, and the name of this river is Aces. Now in old times this river was divided into seven streams, and these watered the countries of the five nations that dwell round about the plain, for a stream flowed through each of the passes. But since the Persians have had the rule of Asia it hath fared otherwise with these nations. For the Great King hath built up the passes of the mountains, and set at each one of them great gates. And so, the water being shut off from the channels whereby it was wont to flow, the whole plain within the mountain hath become a great sea, for the river runneth into it, but has no way by which it may run out. Wherefore these nations, that were wont of old times to use the water, are grievously troubled. In the winter, indeed, they have rain from heaven as do other men, but in summer, when they have sown their millet and sesame, they have need of water. Then as no water is given to them, they come with their wives to the land of the Persians, and stand round about the doors of the Great King, and make a great wailing, and the King commandeth that they should open the doors that lead to the land of those that need the water the most. And when this land hath drunk enough, then the doors are shut, and the King gives command that the doors of those that need rain most of them that are left should be opened. But indeed it is said that the King granteth not the waters till he shall have received great gifts over and above the tribute.

CHAPTER XVI

BABYLON REBELLETH AGAINST THE KING, AND IS TAKEN

When Darius had reigned no long time, the Babylonians rebelled against him, having made very great preparations beforehand. For in the days when the Magian was king, and the seven conspired against him, there being great confusion in the land, the Babylonians ceased not making preparations against this siege, nor was any man aware of what they did. And when the time came that they should rebel openly, they did this thing. Every man chose one woman only out of his household whom he would; and this being done, they strangled all that were left. But their mothers they strangled not, but saved them alive. And the one that each man chose they saved that she might make bread. The cause for which they strangled the women was this, that they might not consume the provisions that they had laid up for the siege.

When Darius heard these things, he gathered all his host together, and marched to Babylon and besieged it. But the Babylonians took no heed of the siege, but went up on the bulwarks of the wall and danced, scoffing at

BESIEGING A CITY

Darius and his army. And as they did so, one of them cried aloud, saying, "Why sit ye here, ye Persians, and depart not? For Babylon ye shall not take till mules shall bring forth foals." These words said one of the Babylonians, thinking that mules should never bring forth foals. And after the space of a year and seven months, King Darius was sore troubled and his army with him, because they could not take the city of Babylon. Yet had Darius used all manner of devices and stratagems against them, and among them the device which King Cyrus had used aforetime, even turning the stream of the river Euphrates; but the men of Babylon ceased not to watch, and he prevailed nothing. Now there was in the army of the Persians one Zopyrus; and this Zopyrus was the son of Megabyzus, who was of the seven that conspired against the Magian. To this Zopyrus it happened in the twentieth month of the siege that one of the mules that carried provender for him bare a foal. But when the tidings of this thing was brought to him, at the first Zopyrus would not believe it. But when he had seen the foal with his own eyes and so was persuaded, bidding his servants tell the matter to no one, he considered it with himself. And when he remembered the words which the man of Babylon had spoken, when the siege was hardly begun, that the Persians might take the city when mules should bring forth foals, it seemed that now Babylon should indeed be taken, for it was of the Gods both that the man had spoken and that the mule had brought forth. Seeing then that the matter had been decreed by Heaven, he came near to Darius, and enquired of him whether the King counted it a great thing that Babylon should be taken. And when he heard that it was indeed so, he considered with himself how he might take the city and gain this glory for himself; for such good deeds are held in high account among the Persians. But after he had weighed the matter for a long time, it seemed that he could by no means bring it to pass, unless he should desert to the Babylonians, having first mutilated himself. After this, thinking it of no account what he should himself suffer, he wounded himself in such fashion as was past all healing, for he cut off his nose and his ears, and laid many stripes upon his back, and so stood before Darius. And when the King saw him so shamefully ill-treated he had great indignation, for this Zopyrus was a man of great repute; and he leapt up from his throne and cried out, asking him, "Who is the man that hath dealt so shamefully with thee?" Then Zopyrus made answer, "There is no man save thee only, O King, that hath power to deal with me after this fashion. And indeed no other man hath done this deed, but I myself have done it. And I have done it because I judged it to be a dreadful thing that these Assyrians should laugh the Persians to scorn." Then the King said, "This is a fair name that thou givest to a very dreadful deed, saying that thou hast thus hurt thyself beyond all healing, because of these Assyrians that we are besieging. For how shall they be vanquished the sooner because thou hast suffered this thing? Surely thou art besides thyself, thinking that this loss shall be our gain." Then said Zopyrus, "I doubt not, O King, that if I had told thee the thing that was in my heart to do, thou hadst not suffered it, for which cause I took counsel with myself alone, and so did it. Now, therefore, if thou fail not on thy part, Babylon is taken. For I will desert to their city, and will say to them that it is thou that hast dealt with me in this fashion. And I think that I shall so work with them that they shall give over to me a part of their army. But thou must do what I now tell thee. Reckon ten days from the day whereon I shall enter their city, and on the tenth day set a thousand men of thy army, being such as thou carest not if they perish, and set them in order by the gates that are called the gates of Semiramis. And on the seventh day after the tenth set two thousand in like manner by the gates that are called the gates of the Ninevites. And on the twentieth day after the seventh set four thousand others by the gates of the Chaldæans. And let these have no other arms but short swords only; these let them have. And when the twentieth day is past, then cause thy army to compass the city round about, but bring thy Persians near to the gates of Belus. For I judge that when

I shall do great deeds for them, the men of Babylon will commit many things to my hands, and among these the keys also of the gates. But after this the Persians and I will order the matter as thou wouldst have it."

Then Zopyrus, having thus instructed the King what he should do, went to the gates, turning himself to see if any pursued, as though he were in truth a deserter. Then they that stood upon the towers, whose business it was to deal with this matter, when they saw the man come near, ran down, and having opened one of the gates a little space, enquired of him who he was and what he wanted, that he came to them. Then he answered that his name was Zopyrus, and that he had deserted from the King to them. Then the keepers of the gates, when they heard these things, took him into the assembly of the Babylonians, wherein standing up he sought to move the pity of them that sat there, affirming that he had suffered from the hands of the King the things which he had in truth done unto himself, and that he had suffered them because he had counselled him to take away his army from before Babylon, seeing that the city could not by any means be taken. "Now, therefore," he said, "O men of Babylon, my coming shall be no small advantage to you and to your city, but to Darius and to his army and to the whole nation of the Persians no small harm, seeing that I know all their goings out and comings in." Zopyrus said this, and when the Babylonians saw the man, how being of great account among his own people, he had had his ears cut off and his nose also, and was marked with many stripes on his body, and covered with blood, they doubted not that the things which he spoke were true, and that he was ready to help them; and so were willing to commit to him all that he asked. Then he asked them to give him an army, which, when he had reviewed, he did according as he had agreed beforehand with Darius, for on the tenth day after that he entered the city, he led forth the army of the Babylonians, and having surrounded the thousand whom Darius had sent from this end, he slew them. But when the men of Babylon perceived that his deeds were like unto his words, they rejoiced exceedingly, and were ready to give all things into his hands. Then again when the appointed days were passed, he chose certain of the Babylonians and marched out of the city and slew the two thousand soldiers that Darius had set in the appointed place. But when the men of Babylon saw this second thing that he did they all praised Zopyrus with one voice. Then the third time, after the twenty days had passed as was agreed, he led the Babylonians to the appointed place, and surrounded the four thousand, and slew them. But after this the Babylonians would have no one but Zopyrus, making him captain of the host and keeper of the wall. Then Darius made his attack as had been agreed; and the men of Babylon went up on to the wall and fought against the Persians, but while they were busy doing this, Zopyrus performed the device which he had devised against them, for he opened the gates that are called the gates of Belus and of Cissus, and let the Persians into the city. And such of the men of the Babylonians as saw that which was done, fled to the temple of Belus, but such as saw it not remained each in his place till these also knew that they had been betrayed.

Thus was the city of Babylon taken for the second time. And when Darius had conquered the Babylonians, he threw down their walls and took away their gates; for Cyrus when he took Babylon the first time had done neither of these things. After this he took three thousand of the chief men among the people and slew them; as for the rest of the Babylonians, he gave them back their city to dwell in; also that they might have wives, for their own they had strangled that their food might not be consumed, he commanded the nations round about to send some of their women to Babylon, appointing a certain number to each, the sum of the whole being fifty thousand.

As for Zopyrus Darius held that no man had done better service to the state, save Cyrus only, for with Cyrus no man among the Persians compares himself. And indeed the King would oftentimes say that he had sooner Zopyrus was healed of his wounds than that he should have twenty Babylons over and above that which he had. And he honoured him greatly, giving him such gifts year by year as are most accounted of among the Persians. Also he gave him the city of Babylon for his dwelling free of tribute.

CHAPTER XVII

KING DARIUS MAKETH WAR UPON THE SCYTHIANS

KING DARIUS, being lord of all Asia, wherein were great multitudes of men and much wealth, purposed to make war against the Scythians, desiring also to punish them for their wrong-doing in time past. Now their wrong-doing had been this. They had invaded Asia in the days of the Medes, and had ruled it for twenty and eight years, and when the years were ended had gone back to their own land. About which going back there is this to be told. When they were come to the border of the land, they found an army drawn out in battle array against them; and this army was of their own slaves. But when they had fought with the slaves many times and could not prevail, one of them said to his fellows, "Men of Scythia, we do ill, fighting against these slaves. Come, let us cast aside our spears and take each one of us his whip. For so long as they see us with arms in our hands they count themselves to be our equals, but when they shall see the whips they will remember that we are their masters." Thus the Scythians did, and it was so with the slaves, that when they saw the whips they fled.

King Darius therefore prepared to make war against the Scythians, requiring soldiers from some nations, and from some ships, and commanding others that they should make a bridge over the Thracian Bosphorus. But in the meantime Artabanus, that was brother to the King, would have persuaded him not to go against the Scythians, as being men that had no possessions; but he could not prevail. And when the King was now about to depart from Susa, which is the chief city of Persia, there came to him one Œobazus, entreating of him that he would suffer one of his sons to tarry at home, for he had three sons and all were in the army. Then the King said that because Œobazus was his friend and asked but a small thing, all his sons should tarry at home. Whereat the man was greatly rejoiced; but the King sent his executioners and slew them all. In this fashion did they tarry at home.

When the King was come to the Bosphorus he set up two pillars of white marble, whereon he inscribed the names of all the nations as many as were in his army; and indeed of all that he ruled none were absent. The writing on the one pillar was Persian and on the other Greek. Now the number of the men was seven hundred thousand, besides those that were in the ships, and of ships there were six hundred. After this he crossed by the bridge, which Mæandrius of Samos had made over the Bosphorus, commanding the Ionians that they should sail along the shore to the river Danube and should make a bridge across the river, and so tarry till he should come. Then he went on his way through the land of Thrace till he came to the river Tearus. Of this

187

river they say that the water thereof healeth diseases both of men and beasts beyond all others. It has thirty and eight springs flowing from one and the same rock, of which some are cold and some are hot. Here the King pitched his camp, and beside the river he set up a pillar by it, whereon was written, "To the Tearus which is the best and fairest of all rivers came Darius, son of Hystaspes, King of the Persians, being the best and fairest of all men." At this time the Getæ, that are called Immortal, submitted themselves to him. This they did without fighting, though they are counted the most valiant and righteous of all the Thracians. The cause wherefore they are called Immortal is this. They believe that they die not, but that such as seem to die go to their god Zalmoxis. And every fifth year they send a messenger to Zalmoxis with a message concerning the things which they need. They cast lots who shall be this messenger; and their manner of sending him is this. Some of them stand in order holding up three spears; and others take the messenger whom they would send to Zalmoxis by the hands and the feet, and throw him from above on to the spears. If the man die they hold that Zalmoxis is gracious to them; but if he die not, they blame the messenger, saying that he is a wicked man; and then they look for another. But the message they give him while he is yet alive. These Thracians shoot arrows into the sky when there is thunder and lightning, and threaten the Gods, holding that there is in truth no god but this Zalmoxis. As for this Zalmoxis, some say that he was a slave in Samos, and that his master was Pythagoras, and that when he had gathered much wealth he went back to his country; and that he affirmed that neither he nor they that were his disciples should die, but should come to a country full of all manner of all good things; and that while he taught these things he made for himself a dwelling under the earth; and that when this dwelling was finished he vanished out of the sight of the Thracians and dwelt therein for three years; and that afterwards he showed himself again to the Thracians, so that they believed all that he had taught them.

After this the King came to the Danube; which when he had crossed, he said to the Ionians that they should loose the bridge and follow him. But when the Ionians were now about to loose it, a certain Coës, who was captain of the men of Mitylene, spoke thus to the King, having first heard that the King would willingly hear his opinion: "This land into which thou goest, O King, hath in it neither fields nor cities; for which reason I would have thee leave this bridge, and leave also them that made it to guard it. For if we prosper in this journey and find the Scythians, then shall we have a way of return, and if we find them not, we shall also have a way. For that we shall turn our backs before the Scythians in battle, I fear not; but only, that not being able to find them, we may wander a long time, and so suffer many things. And I say not this that I may myself be left behind, only I set forth the opinion that I hold to be best for thee, O King; but as for myself I will go with thee, and will not be left behind." These words pleased Darius very much; and he said to Coës, "Man of Lesbos, if I return in peace, come to my house, that I may recompense thee for thy good counsel." After this he took a thong, and tied in it sixty knots, and calling the kings of the Ionians, said to them, "My former purpose concerning the bridge is changed. Take, therefore, this thong, and do thus with it. Loose one knot every day, from the day when I shall depart hence to fight with the Scythians. And if I come not back when all these knots shall have been loosed, then sail back to your own land; but for sixty days, according to the number of the knots, keep this bridge with all the care that ye may." And when he had said this, he went on his way searching for the Scythians.

Now the Scythians, knowing that they could not stand against the Persians in battle, sent messengers to the nations round about that they should help them, for that the Persians had it in their mind to conquer the whole country. And when the Kings of these nations had met in council together, eight Kings in all, the assembly soon divided, for three were willing to help the Scythians, but five were not willing, saying that the Scythians had invaded the land of Asia and were now suffering punishment for their misdeeds. When this was told to the Scythians they considered what they might best do; and it seemed best that they should not join battle with the Persians, but should flee before them, filling the springs and the wells, and destroying the pasture. For this end they divided themselves into two armies; whereof one, being one third part of the whole, having with them also the Sauromatæ, should go towards the river Tanais, if the Persians should pursue them, but if the Persians turned back, should pursue in their turn; and the remainder, having with them the Geloni and the Budini, should go towards the country of the five nations that would not help them, that the Persians might lay waste the country of these nations. But their waggons, wherein their wives and their children are wont to live, and their flocks and herds, save such only as they needed for food, they sent away, bidding them go northwards. After this, the swiftest of their horsemen went forth to meet the Persians, and found them encamped at a place that is three days' journey from the Danube. And when the Persians saw the Scythian horsemen they followed on their track, and pursued them a very long way till they came to the desert. Here Darius halted and made his camp by the river Oarus, and began to build eight great forts. But as the Scythians could nowhere be seen he left the forts unfinished, and marched towards the west. And as he marched he came upon the greater army of the Scythians, and these also gave way before him, having always a day's journey between them and the Persians; and they led them to the towns of those nations that were not willing to help them. All these countries the Persians wasted, save only the country of the Agathyrsi; for these came down armed to their borders, and were ready to fight with the Scythians. And when this had been done many days, Darius, being now weary, sent a horseman to Idanthyrsus, King of the Scythians, saying, "Why flyest thou ever in this fashion? If thou thinkest thyself able to meet me in battle, stay from thy wanderings and fight with me; but if thou confessest thyself to be not worthy, cease from this running, and send gifts as to thy master, even earth and water, and let us talk together." To this Idanthyrsus, King of the Scythians, made answer: "I never feared any man that I should flee before him; and I fear not thee, nor indeed do I now any other thing than that which I am wont to do in peace. But if thou wilt know why we do not fight with thee, hearken: we have neither city nor field for which we should fear, lest they should be taken or plundered, and so join battle with thee. Yet, if thou art minded by all means to fight with us, we have the tombs of our fathers. Find ye these, and seek to destroy them, and ye shall know right soon whether we will fight for the tombs of our fathers or no. But till thou do this we will not fight with thee till we be so minded. And as to what thou sayest of a master, know that our masters are Zeus only, whose son I am, and Vesta, that is Queen of the Scythians. As to these gifts of earth and water, I will not send them; but I will send such as is meet for thee to receive."

This answer the herald brought back to Darius; but when the Kings of the Scythians heard this talk of masters and slaves they were very wroth, and they sent the smaller part of their army to treat with the Ionians at the bridge; but with the larger part they determined not to give way any more before the Persians, but to attack them while they were gathering food. This the Scythians did; and the horsemen of the Persians always fled before their horsemen; but when the foot-soldiers came to the help of the horsemen, then the Scythians gave place. Also they made many attacks on the Persians by night. One thing indeed there was that hindered them. There is neither ass nor mule in the whole land of Scythia; and it often fell out that when the horsemen of the Scythians were pursuing the Persians, the asses in their camp would bray; and when the horses heard it they would be astonished and stand still, pricking up their ears, for they had not heard such sound before nor seen the shape of an ass.

Now the Persians were troubled at what befell them; and when the Scythians saw this, they sought to keep them in their country that they might come utterly to want. For this end they left some of their flocks with the shepherds behind them when they themselves departed to some other place. And the Persians coming upon the flocks and laying hold of them, were much encouraged, and so were the more willing to tarry in the country. But when this had been done many times at last King Darius was in sore straits and knew not what he should do. Then the King of the Scythians knowing this sent a herald with gifts to Darius, and the gifts were these: a bird, and a mouse, and a frog, and five arrows. And the Persians enquired of the herald that brought the gifts what they might signify; but the man made answer that of this he knew nothing, but that it had been commanded him to give the gifts to the King and then depart straightway, but that the Persians might themselves discover if only they were wise, what the gifts signified. And King Darius judged that the purpose of the Scythians was this, to give themselves up to him (which is commonly done by the giving of earth and water), for he considered that the mouse liveth in the earth, and eateth the fruits thereof even as doth a man, and that the frog liveth in the water, and that the bird is most like to the horse, and that as to the arrows these signified their arms which they gave up to him. This indeed was the opinion of King Darius; but the judgment of Gobryas about the matter was widely different. (This Gobryas was one of the seven who slew the Magian.) He indeed interpreted the gift after this fashion: Unless ye become as birds and fly up into the air, or as mice and burrow in the earth, or as frogs and leap into the water, ye shall not go back, but shall be smitten with these arrows that ye die. Thus Gobryas judged about the gifts. But in the meanwhile one of the armies of the Scythians, that which had gone eastward to the Tanais, having returned by the way by which they went, came to the Danube and had speech with the Ionians that guarded the bridge, saying, "Men of Ionia, we come to you offering freedom if only ye will hearken unto us. We hear that Darius when he departed bade you guard the bridge for sixty days only, and that if he came not back within these sixty days, ye should loose the bridge and so depart to your own country. Now if ye do after these words ye shall have no blame either from him or from us. Tarry therefore for the appointed days and afterwards depart." And when the Ionians said that they would do so the Scythians went their way. Then this army of the Scythians departed; and the other army set themselves in battle array against Darius, having both horse and foot, and purposing to fight against him. And it so fell out when the two armies were drawn up the one over against the other, that a hare ran through the midst of the army of the

Scythians, and when the Scythians saw it they left care of the battle and pursued after the hare. And Darius seeing that the Scythians were in much confusion and shouted aloud, enquired what this might mean that the enemy were so disturbed. And when he knew that they were busy pursuing the hare he turned to them to whom he was wont to speak at other times also, and said to them, "Surely these men have a great scorn for us; and surely also Gobryas interpreted the gifts and their signification aright. Seeing then that these things are so, we need good counsel that we may return in safety." And Gobryas said, "O King, I knew before that these men were hard to deal with; and now I know it the more certainly when I see how they scoff at us. My judgment therefore is this: so soon as it shall be night, let us light the fires in the camp, as we are wont to do at other times, and let us tie up the asses in their place, and let us so depart, leaving behind us such as be least able to endure hardship. And let us do this before that the Scythians go to the Danube and loose the bridge, or that the Ionians themselves consider that they may do us this hurt." This was the counsel of Gobryas; and so soon as it was night Darius followed it. He left such of the soldiers as were sick, and such as were of least account, if they should perish, and he caused them to tie up the asses in their places in the camp, and so departed. And the cause why he left the asses and the sick men behind was this: the asses he left that they might make a noise, and the men because they could not make haste in marching. But to these he said that his purpose was to attack the Scythians with the better part of his army, and that they in the meanwhile should guard the camp. This Darius said to them that were left, and having caused the camp fires to be lighted he so departed, and made with all the speed that he could for the Danube. And the asses, missing the noise of the multitude about them, made themselves the more noise, which when the Scythians heard they made no doubt but that the Persians were yet in their camp.

But when the day was come they that had been left behind of the Persians, judging that they had been betrayed by King Darius, surrendered themselves to the Scythians, and told what had been done. And the Scythians, so soon as they heard it, pursued after the Persians with both their armies, and with the nations also that had come to their help; and they pursued, going straight to the Danube. But the Persians and the Scythians fell not in with each other for this cause, namely, that the army of the Persians was for the most part of foot soldiers, and they knew not the way, for indeed in the land of Scythia there are not roads duly made; but the Scythians were horsemen, and they knew the shortest ways. For this cause they fell not in with each other; but the Scythians came to the bridge of the Danube by a long time the first. And when they found that the Persians were not yet come to the bridge, they spoke to the Ionians that were in the ships, saying, "Men of Ionia, the days that were numbered to you are now passed, and ye do wrong still tarrying here by the bridge. And if ye have done this heretofore in fear, fear ye no longer; but leave the bridge with all speed, and go on your way rejoicing, and be free, thanking the Gods and the Scythians for these benefits. And as for the man that was your master, we will so order things with him that he shall not make war against any man hereafter for ever." When they heard this the Ionians took counsel together. Then Miltiades the Athenian, who was King of the Chersonese that is near the Hellespont, advised that they should do according to the saying of the Scythians, and so set the Ionians free. But the advice of Histiæus of Miletus was contrary to this, for he said, "Each one of us is king in his own city by reason of the power of Darius; and if this power be overthrown, then shall we be overthrown also, and neither he nor any man will be King in Miletus, or indeed in any of the cities, seeing that they would all of them wish to be governed by the people rather than be governed by a king." When the other Kings heard this they turned straightway to the opinion of Histiæus, though before they had followed the opinion of Miltiades. And as they judged it most expedient for themselves, so they did forthwith. For they loosed that part of the bridge which was towards the Scythians, and they loosed it for the length of a bow shot. And this they did in order that, though they did nothing, they might yet seem to be doing something, and that the Scythians might not take the bridge by force, and so cross the Danube. And while they were loosing the bridge on the side of the Scythians they affirmed that they were about to do as the Scythians had counselled them. For Histiæus came forward in the name of all, and spoke, saying, "Ye men of Scythia, ye have come to us with counsel that is right welcome, and are zealous on our behalf to good purpose. And as ye have advised us well, so will we serve you faithfully. For we will loose this bridge, even as ye now see us do, and we will work with all our might that we may have the freedom which we desire. Do ye, therefore, while we are loosing the bridge, go and seek for these oppressors, and when ye have found them, avenge yourselves and us also upon them in such manner as they deserve." When the Scythians heard these words they believed a second time that the Ionians spoke the truth, and so departed, seeking the Persians. Yet did they miss them altogether, and for this cause, for which indeed they were themselves to blame, namely, that they had destroyed the pastures and filled up the wells. For if they had not done this thing they could easily have found the Persians. But now the counsel that seemed to have been most excellently devised turned out ill for them. For the Scythians indeed went through their country seeking the Persians where there was food for their horses and wells of water, for they thought that of a surety the enemy would return by this way. But the Persians did not so, but kept to their own trail which they had made marching from the Danube; and so at last, after many things suffered, they came to the river and the bridge. But as they came in the night-time, and the one end of the bridge had been loosed, they were for a while in great fear lest the Ionians should have left them. Now there was with Darius a certain Egyptian, whose voice was louder than the voice of all other men; and Darius commanded this man that he should go down to the edge of the river, and call to Histiæus of Miletus. This he did, and Histiæus heard him call the first time, and straightway brought the ships and joined the bridge, so that the army of the Persians passed over and escaped.

But when the Scythians came again to the river, having missed the Persians a second time, they had great wrath against the Ionians. And from that day they are wont to say of the Ionians, that if they be called freemen then be they the most cowardly and vile of all the nations upon earth, and if they be counted slaves then there are no slaves more mean and worthless.

CHAPTER XVIII

OF THE SCYTHIANS AND OTHER NATIONS

CONCERNING the Scythians and other nations that dwell in these parts there are some things worthy to be told.

All this country is in winter cold beyond measure. For eight months, indeed, the frost is such that a man can scarce bear it; and during this time if you pour water on the ground you cannot make mud; but if you light a fire you can make it. The sea is frozen, and the Scythians march across the ice and drive their waggons on it to that part of Asia which lieth over against them. The sea which they cross is the Cimmerian Bosphorus, being at the extremity of the Black Sea eastward. So is it for eight months of the year; and in the four that remain there is ofttimes frost. Nor is the winter such as is wont to be in other countries; for it raineth scarcely ever, but in summer it raineth continually. Also there is never heard thunder at this time, but in summer it is very grievous. The horses endure the cold, but the asses and the mules perish; but elsewhere asses and mules endure it, but horses if they stand still are mortified by frost. Perchance the cold is the cause why the oxen have not horns. To this agreeth what Homer saith in the "Wanderings of Ulysses"—

"Libya, where quickly grow the lambkin's horns."

For in lands where there is much heat horns ever grow quickly. As to the mules, in Elis also, though it is not over cold, mules are never born. But the people of Elis say that this is by reason of a curse.

As to the feathers, whereof the Scythians affirm the air in the regions beyond them to be full, so that no man may pass through them, or even see them, the truth seems to be this. In the upper country snow falleth continually, but in summer less than in winter. Now, whosoever hath seen snow close at hand when it is falling quickly knoweth it to be like to feathers. And it is easily to be believed that by reason of the cold the northern part of this land cannot be inhabited.

Of the customs of the Scythians the greater part are not to be praised; but one thing they order in a fashion more admirable than do any other men; and this thing is of all human affairs the most important. If an enemy invade their country he shall never escape from it, nor shall he ever be able to come up with them unless they will. For they have neither cities nor forts, but they carry about their houses with them, and they are all archers, shooting from horseback, and they live not by tillage, but by cattle, and their dwellings are on waggons. Hence it has come to pass that no man can conquer them, or even so much as come near to them. For this manner of life the land wherein they dwell is suitable, and their rivers also are a help; for the land is plain and grassy and well watered, and the rivers that flow through it are well-nigh equal in number to the canals that are in Egypt.

They worship five Gods; first Vesta, honouring her beyond all others, and next Zeus and Earth (and Earth they call the wife of Zeus), and in the third place Apollo, and the Heavenly Aphrodite, and Heracles, and Ares. These all the Scythians worship, and the Royal Scythians worship Poseidon. Images and altars and temples they make for Ares only.

They have but one manner of sacrificing. The beast is made to stand with its forefeet bound together. Then he that sacrificeth, standing behind the beast, pulleth the end of the rope wherewith it is bound, causing it to fall; and as it falleth, he calleth aloud the name of the god to whom he offereth the beast. Afterwards he putteth a noose round its neck, and in the noose a small stick, the which he twisteth, and so strangleth the beast. But he lighteth no fire, nor useth consecration, nor poureth out libation; but so soon as it is strangled busies himself with the boiling of it. Now there is no wood in the land of Scythia, for which cause they use this method for the boiling of the flesh. First they flay the beast, and after strip off the flesh from the bones. This flesh they put into caldrons of the country, if they chance to have such; and these caldrons are like to the mixing bowls of the Arabs, but are larger by much; and under they burn the bones of the beast. But if they have no caldron, they put all the flesh of the beast into the paunch, and mixing with it water, burn the bones as before. The bones burn excellently well, and the paunch easily holds all the flesh when it has been stripped off. And when the flesh is boiled, the sacrificer takes of the entrails and of the flesh and casts them on the earth before him; and this is their manner of offering.

But to Ares they offer sacrifice after another manner. In each district of the land, at the chief place of it, there is a temple of Ares; and the temple is of this fashion. Faggots of brushwood are piled together in a heap, whereof the breadth is three furlongs, and the length three furlongs, but the height not so much. On this there is made a platform that is foursquare, and steep on every side save one only; but by this one a man may climb on the top. And on this they pile year by year one hundred and fifty waggon loads of brushwood, for the rains cause it to sink. In the midst of this platform is a sword of iron, made after an ancient fashion; and this sword is the image of Ares. And year by year they offer to this sword sheep and horses; and of the men whom they take captive in battle they choose one out of every hundred and sacrifice them, but after a different manner to the sacrificing of the beasts. "They pour wine on the heads of the men, and slay them over a great vessel, and then taking the blood on to the platform, pour it over the sword that serveth for an image. This they do with the blood, but as to the dead bodies they cut from them the right shoulders down to the hand and throw them into the air. Afterwards they slay the other victims, and so depart.

Swine they use never in sacrifice; nay, they will not so much as keep this beast in their country.

Concerning war they have these customs. The first man that a Scythian slays in battle he drinks of his blood; and he takes the heads of all he slays and carries them to the King. If he carry the head, then hath he a share of all the booty whatsoever may be taken, but if he carry it not, he hath no share. He flays the head in this manner. He makes a cut round about it above the ears, and shakes the skull out of the scalp. The scalp he cleanses with the bone of an ox, and when he has softened it with his hand, useth it for a napkin. The Scythians hang these scalps upon their bridles and make much account of them; for he that hath most napkins of this sort is reckoned to be the bravest of his company. Some sew the scalps together for cloaks, and others make covers of them for their quivers. Now the skin of a man is very white and of a beautiful lustre beyond all other skins. With the skulls they deal in this fashion, but not with all, but with the skulls of these only whom being alive they have most abhorred. The upper part, having been cut off above the eyebrows, they cover with a covering of leather, and use it for a drinking cup. And if a man be poor, this sufficeth him; but if he be rich, he addeth within a lining of gold. If a man have a quarrel with a kinsman, and overcome in a trial before the King, he dealeth with his skull in this fashion. And if he entertain strangers that are men of note, he will hand to them these cups, and tell how they were skulls of kinsmen that had a feud with him and were vanquished before the King.

Once in every year the chief man in each district mixeth a great bowl of wine; and all the Scythians that have slain an enemy in battle drink of it; but they who have not done this taste not of the wine, but sit apart as men that are disgraced. Such as have slain very many enemies have two cups instead of one, and drink from both.

Among the Scythians are many soothsayers, who use divination by bundles of rods which they loose, putting each wand by itself, and so prophesying. If the King of the Scythians fall sick, he sendeth for three soothsayers that are of the best repute. These use divination after the manner aforesaid; and for the most part they say that such and such a man hath sworn falsely by the King's hearth, naming this or that citizen. (It is the custom of the Scythians to swear by the King's hearth when they would take a very great oath.) Then certain men lay hold on the man who is accused of having sworn falsely, and the soothsayers affirm that he has sworn falsely by the King's hearth. But the man is very vehement in denying that he hath done any such thing. Whereupon the King sendeth for other soothsayers, twice as many in number as the former. If these, when they have used divination, find the man guilty of having sworn falsely, then they cut off his head forthwith, and the former soothsayers divide his possessions among themselves; but if the second company of soothsayers acquit him, then the King sendeth for others, and for others again. And if the greater part acquit him, then the former soothsayers must die. The manner of slaying them is this. They fill a waggon with brushwood, and yoke oxen to it; and they bind the soothsayers hand and foot, and put gags in their mouths, and so cast them into the midst of the brushwood. Then they set fire under the wood, and cause the oxen to run, frightening them. Ofttimes the oxen are consumed with the soothsayers, but sometimes, if the pole chance to be burnt through, they are singed only, and so escape. If the King cause a man to be put to death, he slayeth all his male children also, but the female he suffereth to live.

The Scythians make oaths in this manner. They pour wine into a great bowl of earthenware, and after mingle with the wine the blood of them that swear the oath, making a scratch on their bodies with an awl or cutting them with a knife. Then they dip into the bowl a scimitar and arrows and a battle-axe and a javelin, and they say many prayers over it; and after this they that make the covenant drink of the bowls, and their chief followers also.

The tombs of the Kings are in the land of the Gerrhi. So soon as the King dies, they dig a grave, which is very great, and in shape foursquare. Then they embalm the dead body after their fashion, and covering it with wax, lay it in a waggon, and send it to the nation that is next to them. And this again sendeth it on to the next. And every man both of the royal tribe (from whom it cometh at the first) and of the other tribes to whom it is sent, doeth after this fashion. He cuts off a part of an ear, and crops his hair close, and cuts round about his arm, and wounds his forehead and his nose, and runs an arrow through his left hand. So they carry the dead body through the country, coming at last to the Gerrhi, where are the tombs of the Kings. Here they lay it on a mattress in the grave, fixing spears round about it, and putting beams over it for a roof, which they thatch with twigs of osier. In the space round about the tomb (and this is very great), they bury one of the King's concubines, having first strangled her: also they bury his cup-bearer, and his cook, and his groom, and his body-servant, and his messenger, and certain of his horses, and first-fruits of all his other possessions, and also cups of gold—for cups of silver and bronze they use not at all. After this they make over the grave a very great mound, striving with all their might to build it as high as may be.

When a year is passed they do after this fashion. They take the best of the King's servants, all of them being Scythians, and chosen for this office by the King, for they have no servants bought with money, and strangle fifty of them, and fifty also of the best of his horses, and fill their bodies with chaff. Then they fix stakes in the ground, setting pairs of them, and on each pair half a wheel put archwise. On these arches they fasten the horses, and on the backs of the horses they set the young men; and for each horse and its rider there are bit and bridle. Then they range the fifty riders in a circle round about the tomb and so leave them.

When a man of the people dies his kinsfolk lay him in a waggon, and take him about to the houses of all his friends. These all entertain the company at a banquet, wherein they serve the dead man with meat even as they serve the others. For forty days they carry about the dead body and afterwards bury it. And when the burial is finished, then they that have carried about the dead man, purify themselves after this fashion. They set three sticks in the earth inclined together; and on these they put cloth of wool as close together as may be, so making a tent. And in the tent they set a dish, and in the dish stones made red-hot, and they cast hempseed upon the stones. (Hemp groweth abundantly in this land of Scythia, and the people make garments of it that are very like to garments made of flax, so that a man must be skilful in such matters to distinguish them.) Then the Scythians creep under the tent; and the hempseed smoketh upon the stones, so that no bath could smoke more. The Scythians are delighted beyond measure, and shout for joy. This smoking serves them for a bath, for they never wash their bodies with water.

It is an abomination to the Scythians to use strange customs. This may be seen from what befell Anacharsis; for this man, having travelled over many lands, and shown great wisdom whithersoever he went, came to Cyzicus, that is by the Hellespont, as he sailed homewards. Here he saw the people keeping a feast to the Great Mother very splendidly; and he vowed to the goddess that he also would keep a feast to her if he came safely to his home. And having come, he performed his vow, but a certain Scythian saw him, and told the matter to King Saulius, who, when he saw how Anacharsis was behaving himself, shot him with an arrow, and slew him.

So soon as King Darius, having but barely escaped from the Scythians, was come to Sardis, he sent for the two men who had done him good service, to wit, Histiæus of Miletus and Coës of Mitylene. And when they stood before him, he bade them ask a boon of him, each of them the thing that he most wished to possess. Then Histiæus asked of the King that he would give him Myrcinus that belongeth to the Edonians, that he might build for himself a city; for he was King of Miletus. But Coës, being but a citizen, asked that he might be made King of Mitylene. And Darius granted them each his request.

About this time there came to Sardis two Pæonians, who sought to have the pre-eminence among their countrymen. They brought with them their sister, who was a very fair woman and of great stature. And it came to pass one day when the King sat on his throne before the city, that having arrayed their sister in the richest garments that they had, they sent her to draw water for them. So she went, bearing a pitcher on her head, and leading a horse on one arm, and spinning flax as she walked. And the King took note of her as she passed by his throne, for it was not the custom of the Persians, nor of the Lydians, nor of any of the dwellers in Asia, to do after this fashion. And he bade certain of his guards follow her, and see what she would do with the horse. So the guards followed her, and when the woman came to the river, first she gave water to the horse, and afterwards filled the pitcher, and so came back by the way that she had gone, bearing the pitcher upon her head, and leading the horse on her arm, and all the while she span the flax. And King Darius marvelled much at the things that were told to him, and at what he himself had seen. Therefore he commanded the woman to be brought before him; and when the woman came, her brothers came also, for they had been watching the matter near at hand. Then the King asked them, "Of what nation is this woman?" And the young men answered, "We are men of Pæonia, and she is our sister." Whereupon the King said, "Where is the land of Pæonia? and on what errand are you come to Sardis?" The young man answered, "Pæonia is by the river of Strymon, not far from the Hellespont, and our beginning was from the city of Troy, and now we are come to yield ourselves to thee." And Darius asked them, saying, "Do all the women work as this your sister whom I saw?" And the young men answered with all eagerness that it was so; for indeed the whole thing had been done for this end.

Now King Darius had left behind him, when he returned to Asia, a great army of men, eighty thousand in all, with Megabazus for their captain. It was this Megabazus to whom Darius gave great honour by a certain thing which he said of him. For when the King was about to eat pomegranates, and had opened the first, his brother Artabanus said to him, "What is it, O King, that thou wouldst have in such plenty as there are seeds in this pomegranate?" And Darius said, "I had sooner have as many men like unto Megabazus as there are seeds in this pomegranate than be lord of the land of Greece." This man himself said a thing which will never be forgotten by the people of the Hellespont. Being in Byzantium, he was told by the men of the city that the building of Chalcedon was by seventeen years earlier than the building of Byzantium. Which when he heard, he said, "Surely they that built Chalcedon were blind men; for had they not been blind, they had not chosen the worse place for their building, when they might have chosen the better."

When therefore Darius had heard these things concerning the men of Pæonia, he wrote letters to Megabazus, bidding him remove the Pæonians from their own land, and bring them all before him, men and women and children. Straightway a horseman rode with all speed to the Hellespont, and having crossed it, gave the letter to Megabazus, who, having got guides from the Thracians, prepared to make war against the Pæonians.

Now, so soon as the Pæonians heard that the Persians were marching against them, they gathered their host together, and went down to the sea coast, thinking that the Persians would seek to enter their country by that way, and stood ready to meet their enemies. But when this came to the knowledge of the Persians, they took guides, and marching through the upper country before the Pæonians were aware, came down upon their cities, of which, seeing that they found them empty, they easily got possession. And when the Pæonians heard that their cities were taken they were scattered, every man going to his own home, and so gave themselves up to the Persians. Thus were these men with their wives and children taken by force from their native country and led away into Asia.

Nevertheless, Megabazus subdued not all the Pæonians, for, not to speak of others, those that dwelt in the lake Prasias were not conquered by him. He sought indeed to conquer them, but he could not accomplish it. The manner in which they live in the lake is this. In the middle of the water there stand tall piles, and upon these are built platforms, to which there is a narrow access from the land by one bridge only. Now the piles that are under the platforms were planted in the beginning by the whole commonwealth; but afterwards they plant them for themselves according to their law. A man driveth in three stakes (which they bring down from Mount Orbelus) for every wife that he taketh in marriage; and they take all of them many wives. Their manner of living is this. Every man hath a hut of his own upon one of the platforms, and a trap-door into the lake below. Their young children they tie by the foot with a string, fearing lest they should roll into the water. To their horses and their beasts of burden they give fish for food. Of fishes indeed the multitude is so great that a man may open the trap-door and let down a basket into the lake by a rope, and leaving it there for no long time, take it up again filled with fishes. Of fishes there are two kinds, which they call the praprax and the tilo.

Megabazus also subdued the Thracians, concerning whom there are certain things worthy to be told. The Trausi have also this custom. When a child is born, its kinsfolk sit round about it, and lament for all the evils that it must endure now that it is born into the world, recounting all the troubles of human life. But a dead man they bury with much laughter and joy, for they say that he hath been delivered from all manner of unhappiness and is now in great joy and felicity.

Other Thracians have this custom. Each man hath

many wives. And when a man dies there is a great contest among these wives, their friends also taking one side or the other, as to who it was that was most loved of her husband. And she to whom this honour is adjudged, receiving great praise both from men and women, is slain upon the tomb by her nearest kinsman.

Some Thracians sell their children, and buy their wives for great sums of money. To be marked on the body showeth that a man is of honourable station, but not to be marked that he is of the meaner sort. To do nothing is the most honourable thing, but to till the ground the most dishonourable; nor is there anything more glorious than to live by war and plunder.

The Macedonians also submitted themselves to King Darius, giving earth and water.

In those days Aryandes, who was governor of Egypt under Darius, sent an army and a fleet against certain Greek cities which lie to the westward of Egypt, to wit, Cyrene and Barca. (This Aryandes afterwards was put to death by the King, as seeking to get the dominion for himself; for he had coined money, and this money was silver of such purity that there is no other silver like unto it.) Now Cyrene was built by certain men that went out from the country of the Lacedæmonians, one Battus being its founder; and in the fourth generation from Battus there was strife in the royal house; and certain princes going forth from Cyrene built the city of Barca, the Libyans who dwelt in those parts helping them. After this there was trouble again in the cities, Arcesilaüs, King of Cyrene, was driven out for his tyranny by the citizens; and coming back by the help of the Samians executed vengeance upon his enemies with great cruelty. This Arcesilaüs afterwards dwelt in Barca, for he had married the daughter of the King; and the people of Barca, being stirred up by certain exiles from Cyrene, slew him. Now while he dwelt at Barca, Pheretime, his mother, was regent at Cyrene; and when she knew that her son was dead, she fled to Egypt, to Aryandes the governor, and entreated him that he would help her to get vengeance for her son; and she said that the man had been slain because he favoured the Persians. And Aryandes hearkened to her words, and sent, as hath been said, an army and a fleet against the cities. Cyrene indeed suffered no harm, but Barca fared otherwise.

When the Persians were come to the city, they sent a herald demanding that there should be given up to them all that were guilty in the matter of the death of Arcesilaüs. But the people would not hearken to him, for indeed they were all guilty. Whereupon the Persians laid siege to the city; and this they did for nine months, digging mines under the earth, and making attacks upon the city with great violence. As for the mines, indeed, these a certain worker in brass discovered by help of a brazen shield. This he carried about through the city, smiting it upon the ground; and for the most part it was dumb; but where the Persians were digging their mines there it rang. Then the people of Barca dug a mine of their own, and slew the Persians.

But when much time had been spent, and many had been slain on both sides, Amasis, who was captain of the host, devised this device, thinking to take the people of Barca by craft, for force availed nothing. He caused his men to dig by night a broad trench, whereon he laid light planks, and on the planks he put a covering of earth, making it even with the ground on either side. And when it was day he called the men of Barca to a parley; and they gladly hearkening to him, a covenant was made between them. "The men of Barca shall pay a fitting sum as tribute to the King, and the Persians shall not harm the men of Barca." This covenant they confirmed by an oath, which they sware standing upon the planks; and the oath was this, "So long as this earth whereon we stand shall abide, so long shall our covenant endure." Then the men of Barca set open their gates and suffered any of the Persians that would to enter their city. But the Persians brake down the planks that had been laid over the trench, and so held themselves free, for the earth whereon they stood when they sware the oath did not abide.

Then Pheretime executed vengeance on all that had been most guilty in the matter of her son. Nor did she herself come to a good end; for, having returned to Egypt, she died miserably, being eaten of worms; for indeed the Gods have sore displeasure against men when they execute vengeance cruelly.

As for the Persians they came not back to Egypt unharmed, for the Libyans beset them, and cut off all stragglers and such as dropped behind in the march.

So King Darius extended his borders on all sides.

But how he made war upon the land of Greece shall be told hereafter.

www.ingramcontent.com/pod-product-compliance
Lightning Source LLC
LaVergne TN
LVHW011223080426
835509LV00005B/277